PRAISE FOR BELINDA SHEELEY

This book is an intimate journey through unimaginable grief. With the hope of comforting others who are thrust into a life of grief, Belinda courageously shares her memoir. By the grace of God and the strength He provides, she invites you to walk this journey with her and witness how devastation fuels determination, and how grief can coexist with glory, and loss can coexist with hope. Experience blessings along the way that remind us that death separates us by body only and that separation is not forever, but only for awhile.

— STARR GIRDLEY

As a bereaved mother who is learning how to navigate through my own grief journey, *Finding the Joy While Still Feeling the Grief* has been such an inspirational read. Belinda's story is one of great faith and love for the Lord even in her darkest times. The one true joy is indeed in Jesus.

— KATHRYN WIMSATT

I've often heard people tell my sister that she is so strong. She says that she is not, but the Lord she serves is strong. This book has been an example of that. It's not been easy to walk through this again, but it's been a labor of love. Love for her kids and family, and love for the Lord and for the people who she hopes to help by sharing her story.

2 Corinthians 1:3-4

— HEATHER HELLER

After finishing Belinda's book, I could not find the words to express how it touched my heart, so instead I drove to Mt. Eden to simply hug her! I was humbled and honored that Belinda shared her book with me and realize that she was placed in my life and the life of so many others during seasons of hurt and heartache to share God's Faithfulness and the Hope that we have in Jesus Christ, our Lord and Savior. I looked back at a recent text that I sent to Belinda after hearing a sermon on "light in darkness" and wanted her to know that she is a true light, even in the midst of her pain and loss, she is constantly reaching out to others to offer help, support, encouragement, and strength! I have seen her touch so many lives over the years, including my own, and walk with others as they experience the unthinkable.

Whether you are walking through the "Valley of the Shadow" or simply just need to be encouraged, your heart will be truly touched by this incredible family! For anyone who has ever known Belinda, you know that she leads with compassion, care and connection, allowing her faith and strength through Christ to shine through. Her book is a testament of the faith that she holds but also the way she walks in it through the most devastating losses anyone can face. Belinda's raw honesty reveals their pain as they endure the loss of both Joe and Tori but also the love, peace and strength she finds from her faith, her family, and the hope we have in eternity with Him and those we love! The courageous stories shared in this book, the beautiful images of their family, along with her reminder to "Choose Joy" will allow you to see heartache through the lens of hope and leave an impression on your soul!

My heart has been forever touched. Thank you Belinda for being a vessel God can use and continued prayers for you and your family as you minister to others.

— VONDA MARTIN

Belinda and her family have had to walk through the most agonizing pain that I have witnessed in my nearly 30 years of ministry. I believe the suffering of losing a child must be the most excruciating pain that can be experienced in this life. Belinda and Eric have had to endure this suffering not once, but twice!

Witnessing the grace and strength during their loss reminds me of the writings of the Apostle Paul when he writes about the strength of God through weakness, *"But he said to me, 'My grace is sufficient for you, for my power is made perfect in weakness.' Therefore, I will boast all the more gladly about my weaknesses, so that Christ's power may rest on me."* (2 Corinthians 12:9)

As Belinda shares her unimaginable experience of tragedy, you will see this grace and power through weakness in her life. God uses her loss and her darkest time to be the light of Jesus. She uses her weakness to display the power and grace of God in her, and to be a platform of hope.

I know this book was extremely difficult for Belinda as she had to relive the nightmares of her life through pen and paper, but I also know it's her desire to turn her pain into purpose. Belinda's desire is to use her experience to help others in their walk with Jesus. She has already blessed so many through her faith and this book will strengthen your faith.

— CHAD GOODLETT

I needed to read this book, so thank you for sharing. I have so much regret not being around when everyone lost Tori and Joe, and your book provided some healing for me. You have such amazing children and grandchildren. I've always looked up to you like a mom and strive to be like you. I wish I knew why you have had to go through so much. But I do know you have taught me so much and make me want to be closer to God. We have been through a lot together, but I have always loved your family as my own. I will thank God forever for you and what you have done for Elly. I love you so much.

P.S. If I were with you right now I would give you a big hug and probably have your shirt all wet with tears.

— ERICA OFFUTT

FINDING THE JOY WHILE STILL FEELING THE GRIEF

A MOTHER'S MEMOIR SHARING JESUS' HOPE THROUGH TRAGEDY

BELINDA SHEELEY

FISHERS
of **MEN** *press*

Finding the Joy While Still Feeling the Grief

Cover by Madelyn Copperwaite of MC Creative LLC
Layout by Stephanie Feger of emPower PR Group

First edition, March 2024
ISBN: 979-8-218-32449-0
Library of Congress Control Number: 2024901357
Created in the United States of America

Contact Belinda Sheeley at belindasheeley@aol.com for special discounts on quantity book purchases.

Support the Joseph Lee Taylor Sheeley Scholarship Fund with a donation. Contributions can be sent by mail to:

Belinda Sheeley
PO Box 335
Taylorsville, KY 40071

DEDICATION

I suppose most people would dedicate their book to the children they have lost. But since my entire book is centered around them already, I think the dedication should be more about who has gotten me to this point in my journey.

My Jesus, my husband, Eric, my two sons, Ethan and Jacob, and my grandchildren, Waylon, Elly, Tristan and Taylor. These are the people I look at each day and who inspire me to keep my head up and keep going. Jesus entrusted me to care for and be strong for them.

My husband and my two boys were just as devastated as I at our loss, and yet, each day they let Jesus use them to bolster my resolve, my strength. When you can look at someone across a room, a ball field or the dinner table, and know what that person is feeling, it makes an unfathomable bond for life. These men are my gift from the Lord. I am so thankful for each of them for letting me lean on them. They are each wise, kind and so loving.

My grandchildren, also, are blessings to my life. I appreciate God using them to make me keep moving ahead each day.

So, to these family members, I dedicate this book. We are the ones left behind— for now. We are the ones who miss Joseph and Victoria every day. But we are also the ones who are stronger and closer for having loved them!

A NOTE FROM BELINDA

I have heard people say that after you lose a child, you're never the same person again. It's true I will never be the same. But I hope it has made me more caring and more sensitive to other's situations. I pray it has made me a better person.

It seems as though we have lost so many young people in our community lately. I felt like God was leading me to reach out and do something for the other parents that have lost their children. Other people who have lost family members.

When we lost our Joseph in March 2017 and then Victoria in March 2018, I began journaling my thoughts and feelings, sharing some of them on Facebook. Some of my thoughts were kept very private, for my eyes only. But God kept using people—my mother, my pastor, and friends—to encourage me to help others by sharing my journals.

Well, my first thought was that I am not a writer! I made lots of excuses and put off this project, because it was hard to look back at all those feelings again. All those thoughts on paper, on my phone, on the computer—they are still painful and they still hurt.

So, I made God wait. And wait. And wait…

Then something happened that made me realize, God's timing really would have been best (of course). If only I had compiled my journal sooner I could have helped my friend who recently lost her teenage son in a car accident very similar to my son's. I could have handed her this book, and she could have realized she was not alone… that what she was feeling is hurtful and devastating, but normal. That there's a light at the end of the tunnel. That there's still life going on around her, and it's okay for her just to put it all on hold for just a little while to let her heart adjust to living with her son in Heaven.

I pray this journal helps someone else through their sadness and loss. I pray it helps a mom, dad, a brother, sister, grandparent, or friend know it's okay to feel that devastation of grief, but also know God will help us grow from our experience. He is still God and He is in control.

He uses everything that happens in our lives for good. Even when we feel our loss is not fair or the timing was wrong, we have to remember to find the joy in everything that happens. And when we can turn our happy times *and* our sad times over to Him, He will comfort and bless us and love us through every situation.

I feel very blessed to have been shown in several instances the mighty hand of God and true evidence that He is at work among us. My life is quite ordinary, I am quite ordinary… but when I let God use me, then I become someone special! And that is what I want to share with you. In your grief, let God use you, listen for Him, and you will feel Him moving in your life as well.

—Belinda

GOD'S PLAN

March 4, 2017

Hindsight is 20/20 they say. Yes, looking back I can see clearly how everything fell into place by God's hand.

Let me take you back to the night of Joseph's accident. It's important to note that everyone involved in what I'm about to share lives about an hour away from the hospital in downtown Louisville. Yet, everyone was in the right place for us at just the right moment. God would reveal those things to me later though.

We began our evening at my sons' high school baseball fund-raising auction. It was Jake's senior year, and Joseph, a junior, was back on the team after a hunting and fishing hiatus finally! We had such a fun evening together. The boys served chili, helped with the auction items, and worked on the clean-up crew afterwards. And my husband, Eric, and I realized we could have a date night because both boys were going to a birthday party at a friend's house for the night!

It occurred to me that I had my camera in the back of my truck, and I had promised a dear friend that I would take pictures of the Louisville skyline to enlarge and decorate her son's room. Eric really just wanted to head home, but I just had this unexplainable urgency to get this task over with. I had promised it to her weeks prior, but I had not had a chance to do it. That evening was my chance! So, my sweet husband agreed to drive me across the river to take pictures in the middle of the night, despite how tired he was.

WE HAD JUST GOTTEN THE PHOTOGRAPHY EQUIPMENT SET UP AND SHOT TWO PICTURES WHEN MY PHONE RANG.

I didn't recognize the number so I didn't answer. It was late, I had thought… who could be calling me? After the second ring, I got an awful feeling I needed to answer it, so I did. It was my son, Jacob, calling from a friend's phone to tell me he had been driving behind Joe's car and watched him have a wreck. My heart skipped a beat. Jake said it was bad. But he was right there with him.

What were the chances?

The EMS had already arrived. All I could think was I wasn't with my boy. I have a horrible fear for anyone who is in an accident and feels alone. I begged Jake not to leave his brother. The couple who owned the property at the crash site knew our family and came to sit with Joe, offering any help they could.

What were the chances?

Jake promised to stay with Joe, and we ran to our truck to get there as fast as we could. The EMT that was with Joe got on the phone with me and told us to go to the UofL emergency room where they were going to stat-flight him. I quietly told him we would beat the helicopter there since I was already looking at the hospital from across the river.

What were the chances, right?

Turns out, the EMT changed plans and drove him to the hospital instead. I now know they realized how bad he was and suspected he wouldn't make it either way. I didn't know it then, though. I thought perhaps it wasn't as bad as they originally believed so they opted for the ambulance. At any rate, it was wonderful to find out that the EMT taking care of my son at the accident site and on the way to the hospital was a young man who grew up in the church we had attended and actually held Joe as a baby in church on Sunday mornings. And now he held him and comforted him on the way to the hospital as he died.

What were the chances?

As predicted, Eric and I arrived at the hospital before the ambulance. We had time to call our older children, Ethan and Tori, to come down. Jake was already on his way with some friends of ours. I called our pastor, Chad, and his wife. I was a little surprised when they said they would be to us in under five minutes. They were in downtown Louisville at a concert with some other Spencer County friends.

What were the chances?

My mother and her husband had taken my grandmother to dinner that night and were already near the area as well when they dropped her off. So they all came on down together.

What were the chances?

By the time the ambulance finally arrived, it seemed like a lot of Spencer County had shown up in the waiting room with us. We were optimistic for a little while. Then the chaplain called us in to the family room to meet with the doctors. I can remember the doctor's words, can still hear his voice after all this time.

"MRS. SHEELEY, WHAT DO YOU KNOW ABOUT THE EXTENT OF JOSEPH'S INJURIES?"

I knew they said he had shattered his left arm, but that was all anyone mentioned. I just knew he would be so disappointed about not being able to play baseball this season!

"I'm sorry Mr. and Mrs. Sheeley. Joseph didn't make it."

As I'm writing this, my heart is breaking and my tears are falling. But at that moment in time, everything stopped for me. There were no tears. I watched my husband take my daughter, Tori and my son, Ethan, in his arms across the room. I saw my mother and grandmother holding each other. And I saw my sweet Jacob fall to the ground and yell *"NO! Not Joe!"* All I could do was stay calm for my family and not let myself fall apart. That could come later.

I asked God for strength, and I let Him give it to me right then and there. I helped Jake up off the floor and held him. We had to go to the waiting room where all these friends were waiting to hear how Joe was.

It broke my heart to have to tell them this news. There were a lot of tears around me, but God held me together. I think people believed I was in shock, but I wasn't. I was being held up and strengthened, trying to comfort those around me. This was the saddest day of my life, even worse than losing my father years before. But I learned even back then that my sadness was nothing next to the joy that our loved ones experience when they meet Jesus for the first time in Heaven! I had to keep reminding myself of that.

The chaplain came and got us, and let us spend some time with Joseph. She said they had cleaned him up so we could see him. He looked perfect to me. Just as though he was sleeping peacefully. He had the tiniest little scratch on his cheek. That was all. His hair was soft and thick like always. It was my perfect Joe. It was hard to reconcile he wouldn't wake up and grin at me.

Finally, we had to leave the hospital and our boy behind. It was a long ride home. I had to make phone calls to some of our dearest friends to tell them the awful news. When we got home, they were right there waiting for us.

Tori went home to her children to comfort them, and to be comforted by Josh. Ethan had to get little Elly and bring her home to the sad news. I prayed for God to take care of all my grandbabies and help them process the situation. They were all so close with Joseph.

If you can't tell by now, we were all put in a particular place at a particular moment in time so that just when we were needed, everyone was right where they were supposed to be.

What were the chances?

With God in his infinite wisdom and power, there were no chances, no coincidences, no accidents. He put us where we could all do what we needed to do. Be there for each other.

Our family made a difference at the ER. The chaplain sent us a note letting us know how she admired our faith and that she wasn't the only one who noticed it. God used us even in our saddest, most sorrowful moments. If we lean on Him, He will not only bless us and comfort us, but He will also reveal Himself to those around us. How we react in our deepest, darkest moments, our grief, our sorrow—that is our testimony to Christ.

DREAMS

March 6, 2017

Joe has been gone for almost 48 hours. I keep thinking it isn't real. My mind won't let it sink in yet. Part of me knows it, but the other part is waiting for him to walk in the door and tell me this has been the most elaborate "gotcha" of all time. But my other 2 boys have seen the car, or what's left of it. And it's all real. And it's devastating.

But something interesting and unexplainable happened somewhere in the night. I didn't get to start putting the pieces of this curious puzzle together until this evening…

— Belinda

At our house, my oldest son, Ethan, slept on the floor next to the bed of his little girl, Elly, who was just six years old at the time. Just in case she woke and was upset and needing consoling, he wanted to be there. I'd say he needed to be near her for his own peace of mind as well.

Around 5 a.m., Elly woke her daddy and said she'd had a dream about Joe Joe. Elly shared that in her dream, she and her daddy were standing at the front door and saw Joe out front with his car. She said, "He picked me up and gave me a great big hug and told me he would miss me. Then he got in the car, smiled and waved, and a big gold light flashed, and then he was gone!"

Strange that a dream can make a little girl feel comforted so much. She got to see him again! She got to say goodbye! What a gift! But there was more...

My daughter, Victoria, and her three children were living about forty minutes away from us at the time. They came to our home today to be with the family. We all seem to feel better when we're together. Ethan wanted to tell her about Elly's dream, but before he could begin, Tori said something had happened this morning that she had to share with us. Eric, Ethan and I all got chills. I don't think any of us were surprised when she told us what had happened at her house in the early hours of the morning.

She was in her bed, had been trying to sleep, but only managed to doze here and there. Around 3:30 a.m. she was awakened by her ten-year-old, Waylon. He'd had a dream about Joe! Waylon told her how Joe had sat on the side of his bed and talked to him and told him he was okay and lived in Heaven with Jesus now. Tori was so touched by the sweet dream, and she hugged her son and told him Joe was certainly in Heaven, but it was just a beautiful dream. She took him back to bed and tucked him in and kissed him and sat with him until he fell back to sleep.

ABOUT AN HOUR LATER, TORI SAID SHE WOKE WITH QUITE A START!

Her six-year-old son, Tristan, was standing at her bedside with his face about ten inches from hers! She asked him if he was alright... was he sick? Did he need a drink? He just looked at her and said very matter-of-fact, "No, I'm okay. I've just been talking to Joe."

Tori was getting a strange feeling at this point. She hugged him and told him to go back to bed. She said, "Sweetie, it's okay to have good dreams about Joe Joe. He loved you and you loved him. Let's go put you back in bed."

But Tristan surprised her when he said, "No. I want to stay in here with you. I'm sleepy, and Joe is in my bed and he won't quit talking!"

She laughed and said, "Mom, it wasn't a dream—it had to be real! He's right, if it really was Joe there with him, he would have kept talking and kept him up all night telling him stories!"

When I thought about each of the grandkids having a dream about Joseph in the same time frame, it hit me! It would be just like my Joe to make sure the children were okay and that they knew where he was. I have no doubt that he kissed Tori's baby girl, Taylor, and tucked her little blanket around her, as well. He loved our little ones so much, and they all adored him.

I'm thinking these may not have been dreams after all.

AN ANSWER TO PRAYERS

To sleep or not to sleep? I don't think so. It's not that I'm not tired. It's just that if I go to sleep, I know that when I wake up, I will have to realize this nightmare I'm living all over again. So, I doze a little for 10-15 minutes at a time.

We just found out at 10:30 p.m. that Joe was in an accident. He didn't make it. I had a calm about me that I couldn't explain, so I know it was God shielding my heart and keeping me together to do what I needed to do.

But now I'm home at 5:30 a.m. and I know I need to sleep just a minute. Bad idea. When I opened my eyes, I had to re-live it all again.

And it isn't just me. As I lay here in bed staring at my phone and all the messages that people are sending me, I'm kind of jealous that my husband is next to me able to sleep. Part of me wants to be able to sleep too. But then, he gets restless and throws his hands over his face and screams out, "Oh God! He's really gone!" My heart just shattered for him. All I can do is roll over and hold him and cry together. And pray again.

— Belinda

By Monday night, I was worn down. I tried to sleep but when I woke up, I relived it all again. I didn't like this feeling, and I still don't. It's bad enough living with this during the day, but "Please God, I can't keep waking up to this awful truth every day the rest of my life!"

God answered my prayer in an unusual way. He sent teenage warriors to take care of my family: friends of Joe, Jake, Tori, and Ethan. They filled my house during the days (and late, late nights). And when I woke in the night, during those early days it was to the sound of life and laughter in my kitchen. They played cards with my kids. They sang. And they just hung out and listened to music. They were doing what Joe would have been doing.

It's been 3 weeks now. It's gradually getting easier to sleep as the days and nights pass. I can sleep and not have a panic attack from waking up now. My head and my heart are finally wrapping around my loss. It's still so painful, but I can wake now and look over at my husband and just past him, I can see Joe's pictures and think—He's not here, but he's waiting for us. We will be together again soon!

— Belinda

It wasn't just me who struggled figuring out our next moves. My daughter, Tori, alongside the rest of our family and friends, were speechless too. Right after receiving the news of Joe's passing, Tori posted this on Instagram.

How do I do this… How do I let you go? My heart is breaking and I just want to hug you and never let you go. God, I miss you so much… my sweet baby brother. I just don't know how to live without you.

THE FUNERAL

There are so many times I've heard people say, they couldn't remember things from the funeral for their family members. They were so overwhelmed by grief and sadness that everything was a huge blur to them. I am thankful beyond words that is not the case for my family. I remember tons of moments from the visitation, the service, and the burial of my son, Joseph. So many dear people gathered around us, praying for us and supporting us. I can still remember much of that time.

I remember the precious little four and five year-old T-ball players that Joe helped with coming to say goodbye to him as they carefully laid their Minions baseball caps in the casket with their coach. Such a sweet but sad moment.

WHILE IT WAS A SORROWFUL TIME LOSING A CHILD,
THERE WERE MOMENTS WHERE I COULD FEEL HE WAS
RIGHT THERE WITH US, TRYING TO RELIEVE OUR SADNESS.

In his life, Joe's mission was to make people laugh and find the humor or joy in everything. He did love a good practical joke. So, it was the case as we prepared for the funeral.

It was common knowledge that Joe was forever "borrowing" his dad's and his brothers' shirts, often without asking. But he most always put their stuff back and no one seemed to mind. But on the day of the funeral, we all looked at Joe and looked at Eric kind of puzzled. I said, "Honey, isn't that your shirt Joe Joe is wearing?" We just smiled at each other and had a private little laugh that the funeral director did *not* understand.

You see, my mom had gone to our house and gotten in Joe's closet and brought down what she thought was Joe's shirt (it *had* been in his closet after all).

So, we just did what we thought would make Joe happy— Eric wore Joe's shirt to the funeral service, and I'm sure it made Joseph tickled to see us chuckling about it. A "Joe Wink" from Heaven… maybe?

Later at the visitation, after standing in the receiving line for over eight hours, Eric and I were getting a little tired. We finally let our friend, Michelle, escort us out for a break—fresh air and a drink were much needed. We were both aching to sit down. There were so many people in the funeral home, we couldn't get through the crowd so she had us go through a door I hadn't noticed before. It was the door to the flower room located right behind where we had been standing. It was nice and cool in there, and there were chairs! There was another door leading to the outside back of the building, but when Michelle went out it, it closed. And it locked! Yes… we were locked in the flower room right behind our son. That was definitely a "Joe Wink" moment. We sat there for a long moment, then looked at each other and laughed out loud! This could only happen to us. I looked up and said, "Good one Joe! Now send someone to open the door please!"

It took a while but, Michelle finally came back to retrieve us. Oddly enough, we needed that moment to look at each other and laugh.

We needed to feel Joe with us. And we needed the comfort that it gave us. God blessed us with these "Joe Wink" moments that would have made him bust a gut laughing at us. And that was worth a lot to us! It made it feel like he was still right there with us.

YOU NEVER KNOW WHO IS WATCHING YOUR REACTIONS DURING A CRISIS.

You could cause someone to see their own experiences in a different way. I didn't realize, but that very thing happened to my family during Joe's funeral.

A lady approached me in tears at the funeral home. I knew she loved Joe; she saw him frequently when he came in her store for breakfast before school. I hugged her and thanked her for coming and being with us. Then she kind of shocked me. She thanked *me*! *What*?!

She told me how almost a year ago she had lost her brother. She shared that her and her family hadn't handled it well. There was still lingering anger and resentment at him being taken so young. She told me, "I keep looking at you all standing here, consoling people, smiling and sharing memories of Joe. It dawned on me that my family could have handled things a lot differently this past year. But it's not too late to change."

I was blown away. God used us to touch her heart and make her perspective change. She chose that moment with me to see things in a happier light. And I honestly saw the weight lifted off her shoulders when she hugged me again.

I rarely feel gifted in knowing what to say to people. I am not what I would consider a fount of wisdom. But at that moment, not many words were needed except, "I know you and your family loved your brother, but would you wish him back from Heaven? From being with the Lord? God gave you so many good memories with him while he was here—don't let being apart from him ruin all your happy times together!"

Even though it was hard getting through those initial sad days of losing Joe, I leaned hard on the Lord and asked Him to bless my family and comfort us and use us.

If you are grieving, let God strengthen you and guide you so that even in your despair and darkest times, others can see Him in you. You may make a life-altering difference in someone's life. Your testimony could be what they need at that very moment in time to cause them to find Jesus.

I had the honor of writing the eulogy for Joseph's funeral service.

Joseph came into the world special. He was born in the car on the way to the hospital at 90 miles an hour on I-64 as we passed Southeast Christian Church at 5 a.m. His daddy drove fast as the car would go to Kosair Hospital where our premature little baby had to stay for about 6 weeks in the NICU. The doctors said he may not grow to be as big as our other children. Well, turns out that Mt. Eden air and Momma's cooking, and chores with Daddy brought him along just fine, right? Our baby passed us all up!

Every time Eric and I think of our life with Joe, we just can't think of anything we would like to do differently. There are only really happy memories. Memories of all of us fishing and hunting together; taking trips to the lake together; going to endless baseball games—so many we can't begin to count. I can't think of one thing in our life with Joe that we would change—and that's a blessing to be able to have that peace right now.

Joseph had an unending lineup of friends. And it's a very eclectic group. Funny to think that our big old sweet-hearted, country-twangin' overall-wearing boy had friends from every possible group from rednecks to athletes to preschoolers to the Old-timer's breakfast club at the Dairy Queen. He liked and cared for all kinds of folks.

Joseph was a protector of his friends and a champion for the underdog and, of course, ladies everywhere. He came home from school several times and said "Momma, Daddy—well it's like this. You probably are gonna be getting a phone call about me from my teacher." And then proceed to tell us how he had to stop someone getting picked on. And he may be in a bit of trouble, but it was for a good cause. As a parent it's a little hard to get upset with your boy for having someone's back. We were pretty proud that he cared about folks enough to stand up for them.

Eric and I taught all our kids about honor—about shooting straight with folks and keeping your word. Being trustworthy is becoming scarce nowadays. But Joseph was. He was someone you could count on. And had a big kind heart too.

Joseph was baptized by Brother Tom at Mt. Moriah Church when he was five-years-old. Of course, he said it wrong—he said "Bapti-tized." Tom tried to work with him on the pronunciation to no avail. But Tom said comprehension was more important than pronunciation. Joe loved that everyone in his family was saved and knew Jesus in their heart. "That way," he said, "we will all be together in Heaven." "And then we will have each other forever." That's the best thing any momma could ever hear.

Joe was an old soul from early on. As a little boy he gravitated towards the older gentlemen at church to hang out with. He loved hearing their stories so much. Which now that I say that, it explains a lot why he sounds like Jerry Clower telling his stories now.

Not a day ever went by that Joe didn't hug his Momma and Daddy and flash that big old smile. And I don't know why but even though he would need fussing at sometimes, it was really hard to stay mad at the boy.

His happiness was infectious—so you know that comes from the Lord. Joe could change your mood just by walking into the room with that big old goofy grin, as Ethan called it. It literally was Joe's mission in life to make sad folks happy and happy folks crack up laughing.

He was a true outdoorsman—not much on video games or even TV really. Just happy being in the outdoors. He loved pond fishing or frog gigging with his sister or his buddies. He was happy on the lake fishing with his dad and brothers and Grandpa Doug. So happy that he kept begging the high school for a BASS Team, and of course he finally got it. He loved deer hunting of course. But after his buddy introduced Jacob and Joseph to coon hunting, all our lives changed forever. I can tell you, there is one sad lonely Walker hound at the Sheeley house right now waiting for her Joe to take her on a run. I swear I think I can hear her cry at night with us.

Joe was such a hard worker. For just being 16 he had already worked for half his life. His first real job was at the greenhouse across the road. Then he worked in tobacco for anyone in Mt. Eden that would hire an eight-year-old. He loved working this past fall at Markwell's in Glensboro processing deer during hunting season. He must have been pretty fair at the skinning part—but we wonder if poor Denny and Joan knew what they were getting when they got Joe. Joe would tell every customer that dropped off some funny story before they left. Maybe Denny and Joan hired him for his enter-tainment value as well?! And Miss Joan kept him well-fed so we suspect he enjoyed that more than the whole work part. His summer job at NTS was hot and hard. Landscaping, lawn maintenance—whatever was needed, Joe did it. And he loved the hard work. We are so glad Joe took pride in doing his best—no matter what his job was. We tried to instill a good work ethic in our kids and Joe definitely made us proud.

His most recent job was at the Country Mart here in town. He wanted to save up enough to buy a new truck to haul his dog around hunting. Ally and Tyler were so good to give Joe the opportunity to work there. And it wasn't a hard job—but Joe's job had rewards. I loved hearing him say "Momma, give me a hug—I'm headed to the Country Mart." Then He would come home and tell us all the people he saw each day. He met new folks each day and by the time he walked them out with their groceries he felt like he had made a new friend. And it really was just that simple with Joe.

Joe and Jacob have played baseball since they were in kindergarten. Usually on the same team. He played in Spencer and Shelby Counties over the years—and made lifelong baseball family ties with each team he played with. You won't believe this but the Shelby County folks thought Joe had a country accent. So much so, that they called him "Big Country". Joe took a break from baseball after middle school to further his hunting ambitions.

And, of course he leant his talents (and patience) to coaching his niece Elly's baseball team, and teaching pitching to the SCYBA Pirates players. But this past summer he got baseball fever again and asked Thad if he could come back and play. He was so excited to be pitching. Even when he caught the ball with his nose and fractured it a few weeks ago, he couldn't wait to get back to playing this coming week. Joseph and our whole family have been blessed by a long list of amazing coaches over the years. And Coaches Kingsolver and Slaughter are right at the top. And Joe's teammates have been so amazing supporting and encouraging each other. You've suffered one loss this season guys in losing #22 this week. Now he will expect you to take his brother and rally around him and love each other and play like he's watching every game. Cause he will be.

Joe had a unique relationship with many of the teachers and staff at the school. Joe loved school for the people and relationships. Not so much the school work, but hey, that's just Joe. From Mr. Adams and Mr. Hahn and every teacher and staff member who ever worked with Joe his family wants to say a big special—"WE'RE SORRY". So many of you have shared your Joe experience with us and it often starts with "Joe please go to class —aren't you late again?" Or "please don't throw mints at my head in my class". And then ends with laughter. But, really, we are so grateful beyond words that each of you helped mold our boy into a unique young man. You all are so appreciated.

Joseph is the youngest of 4 children. And they are a tight knit group of kids. But I gotta say, when the nephews and nieces started arriving, Joe was in Heaven. He said nothing was sweeter or cuter than our family's babies. He thought they were angels from Heaven. And he was close with each one of them. Waylon and Tristan loved Joe spending the night and having smack-down wrestling matches, light saber sword fights and building Legos. Then he could change gears and play Monster High dolls and makeup and baby dolls with Elly. Then turn around and hold baby Taylor and make goofy faces to make her laugh. I think he appealed to just about every age group. Just something about our Joe.

Since it was Joe's goal in life to make people laugh and be happy, his family wanted this day to honor that. It's hard to find the happy when we're all hurting so much, but to honor Joe I think we should make him a promise today. For the rest of the day, try to tell a "Joe Story" to someone to make them smile and lift them up. I don't think God allows his folks in Heaven to see anything unhappy down here. So, if we all try to be happy together here at some point today—Joseph will get to look down and see us and how much we all love him. And I bet we feel his presence just a little every time we laugh.

Tori added comments to Joseph's eulogy as well.

I have so many wonderful stories that I could share about my amazing brother. It's almost impossible to pick one. My most cherished memories of him will simply be all the times I sat listening to his stories.

When Joe would come to stay the night with me, he would literally talk from the time I picked him up, to the time I dropped him off. Then he would call me before I got to the end of the road because he remembered just one more thing he needed to tell me!

My favorite thing about Joe's stories was that they always had something to do with our brothers. Ethan and Jacob were always his role models and best friends. All of our visits and times together ended with a big ole bear hug and every phone call or text ended with an "I love you Sis…"

I'm sure gonna miss that sweet country twang in his voice.

Many people shared kind messages on Joe's memorial Facebook page. A portion of our church wore flannel shirts that week to our church's service to honor Joe. I was so thankful to everyone for letting our family know how much they love us and remember our Joe Joe.

Our family would like to thank you from the bottom of our hearts for your sweet thoughts and prayers as we go on without our Joe Joe. Although we miss his laughter, smile and love, we know he lives forever in Heaven with Jesus, waiting for us to join him in God's time. We also know that Joe will continue to live on here in your smiles and hearts when you think of him or tell a "Joe" story. We can feel you praying for us and we appreciate that more than words can say. Thank you for honoring our sweet boy. And thank you for all the visits, the cards, the wonderful food, the precious, thoughtful gifts - but, mostly for loving on our family in our time of loss. It is our prayer that Joe touched someone's life in such a way that they will come to know Jesus and have a relationship with Him. We pray that God will continue to use Joe's memory to inspire everyone whom he met.

The Sheeley Family
Eric, Belinda
Tori, Ethan, Jacob
Waylon, Elly, Tristan and Taylor

MY SURVIVAL GUIDE TO GRIEF

After suddenly, unexpectedly, tragically, losing my son, Joseph, three weeks ago in a car accident, I have learned some things about the grieving process that I never thought about before.

— Belinda

Like many things in life... grief is full of choices. It can be dealt with positively or negatively. It can be about me and my needs and my loss, or it can be about the great memories of Joseph. I can cry and hide away in my house or I can get out and help other people with their needs. It can wipe me out at the knees or it can lift me up.

The point is... I can choose.

And so, I choose to be positive. My loss can be used to glorify God if I allow Him to work through me. My pastor says "God is a gentleman and He lets us choose whether or not we let Him in our heart. He doesn't force His way in." The same is true here. He can ease my grief only if I ask it of Him, and then *believe* that He will, and then *allow* Him to.

I CHOOSE FOR MY GRIEF TO BE ABOUT MY SON—NOT ABOUT ME.

Even to this day, each time I think about "my" loss and what "I'm" missing out on with Joe, I get really sad. However, when I think about Joe and the many crazy, funny, wonderful memories he gave me, I can smile when I think about him. I love it when people tell me stories about my boy. They always lift me up and make me smile.

I've had people tell me they are so sorry that he died so young; that we only got to have him for sixteen years. Hmmm… I learned early on to tweak that statement just a bit and I tell them, "No—we *GOT to have him* for **sixteen** years! And they were really, *really* good years!"

I CHOOSE FOR MY GRIEF TO BE USED IN A POSITIVE WAY FOR OTHERS.

If I stay busy helping someone each day and showing them the kindness that Jesus showed—the kindness that my son always displayed—then I don't have time to wallow in sadness. And at the end of the day, I can feel good about seeing the evidence of not only my good deeds, but also the positive impact my son's life is still having on others.

Do I miss Joe? Yep—*like crazy*—every day. I sometimes feel like I have a huge hole in my gut and I can't breathe. But then, I remember he's not really gone. He's just somewhere else waiting for me. And I remind myself now is the time to *believe* what I believe in.

Do I still cry for me? Yes, because I miss his smile and his hugs, and his very presence. I don't wish him back from Heaven though—that wouldn't be fair.

Am I still grieving? Yes, I am, but on *my* terms with *God's* help.

I choose to NOT let Satan overrule my memories of my son. After all, I look forward to seeing Joe again. And that is God's comforting promise to me.

Joe's favorite Bible verse was Philippians 4:13: "I can do all things through Christ who strengthens me." This is how I know I can make it through each day… with Jesus by my side.

Not long after he died, I posted this on Facebook. Joe's friends did some burnouts in front of our house in honor of Joe.

Someone paid Joe a visit today—thank y'all for thinking of him (and us). Hope y'all had a good, safe ride. It was a beautiful day for it. Who knew black lines on a road could make a Momma and Daddy so happy lol. Love each one of you to pieces!

THE HALLWAY

I hate looking down my hallway.

I sit in the living room in my spot on the couch and my head plays tricks on me, thinking he is coming down the hall. But he never will again.

The most simple, mundane things are absolute agony.

Hearing a car pull in the driveway. Not Joe.
Hearing the phone ring. Not Joe.
Hearing the basement door open and close. Not Joe.

I pray I get used to this soon. It's an awful thing to look down the hallway over and over again thinking Joseph is gonna open that door and come in and hug me before he leaves.

— Belinda

I may not have Joe, but I have precious memories. All of my boys worked on farms at some point. I never could convince them to leave their boots outside or even on the mat inside that I set out for them. So, I adapted and just tried to pick my battles, and they would help clean the floor—eventually.

JOE WAS SO GOOD AT ALLEVIATING MY AGGRAVATION.

He knew he should take the boots off, but when he was in a hurry just to pick up something from his room and run out again real quick, he would yell at me all the way down the hallway, "I love you Momma! I love you Momma!"

Like that was gonna make me **not** notice his dirt trail!

I reckon he was right though, because when someone 6'3" is stomping through the house yelling "I love you Momma!" it just tends to make one laugh—hard. Have I mentioned he loved to make people laugh?

I even chased him up the hallway with the broom one day and he turned around, grabbed me up, kissed me and kept hollering his "I love yous" till he got back outside.

I'd sure love to hear that voice, hear those boots stomping up my hallway, see the dirt trail, and hear the laughter coming out of that boy.

I am so thankful for the vivid memory of it all.

BE HAPPY

Even now, sometimes folks are afraid to mention Joe in front of me.

I think they don't want to upset me. It's okay though. Don't be afraid to make me cry talking about Joe. Honestly, I will probably cry and smile at the same time because each time somebody talks about him, it's usually a sweet memory or a funny story. And I really love it when people tell me a "Joe" story that I haven't heard yet.

I spent most of Joe's sixteen years laughing at him or with him. He was our little entertainer, telling stories like his hero, Jerry Clower. I don't know why, but from a little bitty fella, he wanted everyone laughing. He was happy and wanted everyone else to be happy as well.

I remember a few years prior to his death when we were getting ready for our Florida trip, I downloaded a bunch of songs I thought would be fun to have at the beach. One was *Don't Worry Be Happy* by Bobby McFerrin. Joe cracked up so hard when he heard it the first time. He said, "Where has that song been all my life?!" Now that I think of it though, that was exactly his attitude toward life!

Don't worry about the little things that come along, just be happy.

A CLOUD

May 12, 2017
Instagram Post from Tori

I'm generally not a super emotional person. But dealing with tragedy can change a person I suppose.

With that said, sometimes it makes me feel better to talk out loud to Joe. I don't know why, but it does. I guess I've just subconsciously been waiting for a response.

Well at the end of a very one-sided conversation the other night, I said, "I sure do love and miss you baby brother." Then I turned around and saw this.

Yes, I know it's just a cloud. But to me, I could/can see a heart and its pink... kind of made me feel like he was saying he loved me too... take it for what it's worth, but it made me happy.

THE ABC'S OF JOE JOE

On May 12, 2017, Tori wrote the ABC's of Joe Joe for her children who were missing their Uncle Joe. We had no idea she would be gone as well in less than a year.

The ABC's of Joe Joe

I know Joe Joe is in Heaven. But mommy what does that mean?

Quite simply son, he gets to see everything you have seen!

He will watch you bite an APPLE that may cause you to lose a tooth.

He is with you at BEDTIME, watching over you.

He'll laugh in heaven as he watches you playing in the CREEK.

He'll need you to play with his hound DOG now cause he's used to hunting every week.

Joe would want you study and have a good EDUCATION. He always said he was smarter than me! And he knew that was what you needed to have for a good foundation.

FISHING was one of his favorite things to do. So when we go, you better believe he is there too!

GOD *was his Lord and Savior. And for that we give praise. That means we have the promise of seeing him again someday.*

HAPPY *is how we remember him. Even if we feel a little sad. Joe wants us to do this, he wouldn't want you to feel bad.*

INSIDE *your heart is where his memory stays. Thinking of him helps me pass time through the days.*

JOKING *is one of the things he most loved to do! I'm pretty sure that's who taught all those corny jokes to you.*

With KINDNESS *is how he treated everyone he met. Joe would teach you how to shake hands and look people in eye when you first met.*

LOVE *is what you feel when you think of him. He would drown you in love, good thing you know how to swim.*

MISSION *trips to jungles! That was one of his dreams. To spread God's word to others. Even if it scared me enough to want him to stay home with his baseball team.*

NEPHEW. *That's never what he called you though. You were his little buddy and friend! Oh, the trouble you two got in!*

OPEN. *That was the constant state of his heart. Please keep him in yours. He is in mine. So, we never have to part.*

PERFECT *is how he described his teeth after the dentist took off his braces. But then he went and broke his nose in several different places!*

QUALITY *is how I would describe the type of man he was becoming. Even if some may say he was prone to frivolity.*

RESPECT *is how he treated his elders. He must have learned a thing or two from the old men he knew that were welders.*

SMILING *is how you would always see his face. If you were having a bad day, that smile could change the whole days pace.*

Joe *was always* THOUGHTFUL. *He considered others before himself. Will you do that as you grow up? Will you put others before yourself?*

He *had a good* UPBRINGING. *Granny and Papaw saw to*

that. *They went to almost every baseball game. They loved when he was up to bat.*

VACATIONS *with his family were a fun thing to do. I will take you to some of his favorite places. This I promise you.*

WONDERFUL *is always how we will remember him. Do you remember how we used to all go to the pool to swim?*

Joe Joe *was kind of clumsy. He broke bones which meant he had to get XRAYS. Do you think he learned to be clumsy from me? He very well may!*

YOUNG, *he was only sixteen-years-old. But it seems that born with an eighty-year-old soul!*

The ZOO *is where he told you they would lock you up and make you stay. He said you were a monkey, and even though he was just joking, you got scared and tried to run away.*

Oh, my sweet little one. Hold your memories close and dear. Our Joseph is always with us. And should you feel lonely, read this to yourself. Say your ABC's of Joe Joe. I promise he will always be near.

— TORI

THE HEADSTONE

Yesterday my family and I were invited to a cookout by a group of teenagers who knew Joseph and considered him their good friend. I had met some of them through school over the years. Some I had never met till after Joe's death. But they all seemed to hold Joe in high regard.

When I told some folks where I was going today and who I was going to be with, I got some raised eyebrows and a few stories about the backgrounds and lifestyles of the kids I was going to see. I was told they were a rough crew. But, Joe saw something so special in these kids – and today I saw it too.

— Belinda

These young people that were so close to Joe took it upon themselves to design and create T-shirts, truck decals and bracelets in Joe's memory. They took orders and sold these items to raise money to help our family and to honor their friend.

They had a cookout to present to Eric, Tori, Ethan, Jake, and me our "Joe shirts" and the money they had raised for us to pay on Joe's funeral expenses—$1,200. They were so proud to give it to us, and they told us they wished it could be more.

YOU COULD HAVE KNOCKED ME OVER WITH A FEATHER
THAT DAY.

For a minute, I was speechless. Then I gathered myself and held up
that blessed wad of cash. I smiled at them and said, "You don't even
know it, but God has been using you all this week. You couldn't
possibly know this, but this amount, right here in my hand, this was
the exact amount that we needed to pay the balance on Joe's headstone. And I didn't have any idea where I would scrape together that
much cash."

Of course I couldn't hold back the tears.

I thanked them and told them that God had used them to minister
to our family. Those were some emotional kids—about fifteen tough
looking guys and gals with wet eyes. That amount was not a coincidence! I believe God used that circumstance to show all of us that
He is working in all of us.

> They were respectful and so sweet and kind. And when they
> took us in to the house to eat, these kids—who might not
> pray regularly—asked me to have the blessing for our food. I
> was so touched and blessed that they were so open to hear
> what I shared with them.

I know God was and is working on these young people. We invited
them to come to church with us. A few were afraid the walls would
fall if they came. A few were worried about not being dressed right.
But we told them our church was a little different than most and
that they could come in jeans and T-shirts and everyone would love
them just as they were. They found that hard to believe, but it's true
and that's why I love my church.

If you ever visit Joe's grave, know that a lot of love and hard work
went in to that headstone. It was paid for with love and determina-

tion of really great kids, paying respects to a friend that left them just a little sooner than expected.

I just learned that one of the young men in this crew, with whom I've become very close, just added another new addition to his family. Not only does Sammy have a lovely wife, Molly, and two beautiful little girls, Kimber and Madilyn, but now he has (wait for it… drumroll please) Baby Joseph. My heart could just burst with joy right now! Thank you Sammy for honoring Joe and blessing our family in such a special way!

JOE'S MARK

Like your short time here on earth,
From the time of your birth,
Didn't have to know you a long time,
For that was enough for you to shine.
Yes ma'ams, no ma'ams were so much your style,
Proving an upbringing going the extra mile.

As did the way you looked out for others,
Making all feel like they too were brothers.
But inseparable and like a twin, Jacob,
Knowing for him your heart beat a special throb.
Always the son, grandson, brother, uncle and special friend,
Loved by all as well that famous way you grinned.

Knowing now that there in Heaven with God,
You're rushing to help the next with that reassuring nod.
Just as here on earth you so proved your worth,
Now our "Joe" up high will continue to go forth.

—JOAN MARKWELL

Joan and her husband, Denny, own Markwell's Deer Processing. They hired Joseph to work for them for the fall and winter season prior to his death, and I'm not sure really how much deer he skinned or if he just stood and told the customers and workers stories. But I'm told he kept them all in stitches, so I'm going with the latter.

He was well loved there, and he loved Denny and Joan in return. Everyone who comes in contact with our kids leaves a mark in their life. How blessed that God put good folks like the Markwell's in our lives.

ETHAN'S WRECK

It's been 6 weeks since we lost Joseph, although it feels like just a few days. Like time is standing still in my head. I go through the motions daily, but my mind is on hold. I try not to let it show, but if you're close to me, you know I'm deep in my thoughts. Sleep still eludes me—or I try to elude sleep is more accurate. But eventually it finds me and I drift off.

In one of my sleeping moments, I heard the phone ring next to me. No one ever calls at 6 a.m. with good news, so I was a little nervous to answer the phone. It was my husband, Eric. And the first thing out of his mouth was, "Ethan has had a wreck—but he's okay." When I finally let out the breath that I didn't realize I had been holding I informed him that was not the correct way to present that news! First you say, "Ethan is okay, totally fine, not hurt at all and oh, by the way he had a wreck."

— Belinda

We were all so relieved.

Eric and Ethan had both been on their way to work, both heading out different ways, yet somehow Eric got to him quickly. By the time I got up, they told me to just meet them at the auto body shop where the truck was towed.

My first look at Ethan was unbelievable. Not one scratch on him anywhere.

The truck was not so fortunate! It had flipped completely over and there was not one piece of that vehicle that wasn't damaged. Even the inside of the truck was buckled and messed up.

I asked Ethan if he had been wearing his seatbelt. The look on his face was answer enough. No seatbelt. Before I could ask my next question though, he told me how it happened.

It had been raining earlier that morning and as he went around a sharp curve, the tool box in the bed of his truck came unbolted and slid hard to the side. The road had some oil on it, and combined with the rain and the force of the tool box, the entire truck slid across the road flipped into a ditch and landed upside down.

Well then, that explained the sod on top and in the bed of the truck. So, my next question naturally was, "How did you not fly out of the truck or get smashed in there?"

He said something incredible next. "Joe was with me, Momma. He held me in my seat." Ethan could actually feel something or someone holding him tightly in the driver's seat.

I didn't know what to say except, "Thank you Jesus for sending Joseph to be his Ethan's guardian angel this morning." I do believe that the Lord lets our loved ones help take care of us. And I am so grateful for that.

A RIDE WITH JOE

This was a Facebook post by Niki, whose son played baseball with Joe. It so amazing and incredible and evidence that God is allowing Joe to be with us.

I wanted to share this because it's pretty special. Quite unbelievable, and we know the reason why. If you do not believe we have angels among us, maybe you will think twice.

My son was driving along yesterday, and he started to smell smoke and his seat got extremely hot all of a sudden. He looked out his window and flames were coming up the side of the door. It was engulfing as he was driving! He pulled off, and jumped out. Thankfully he was okay. The truck was not okay. It took a bit to get the fire out and everything, and as you can see, was burnt where he was sitting... except, this handkerchief.

You see... Bailey lost a special friend last year. Sixteen-year-old in a car accident, Joe. He grew up with him, played ball with him, got his driver's license with him, etc.

Yesterday, Bailey was on his way to attend a "Ride for Joe" when this fire started. Tomorrow will be the one year anniversary of Joe's death. That handkerchief was untouched while everything around it burned. One of our ball team moms made the handkerchiefs for the ball players for Joe's funeral.

I think Bailey did have a passenger yesterday. He literally had "A ride with Joe."

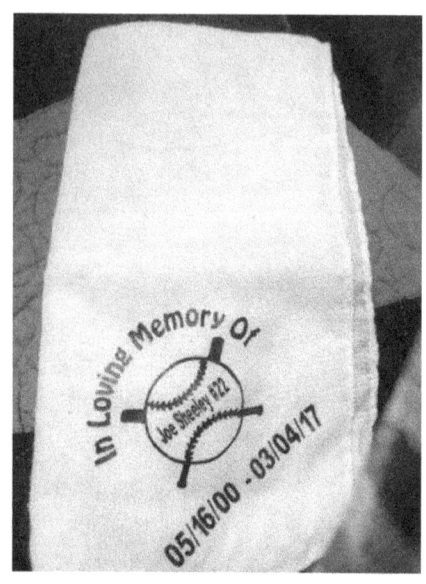

HOMERUN FOR JOE

The following is a newspaper article that was written and published in the *Spencer Magnet Newspaper*.

A HOMERUN TO CHERISH
Sheeley says late brother helped power his first HR
By John Shindlebower

Jacob Sheeley has cleared the fences in practice and in summer league games, but not in a varsity game. So, on Monday night, in the bottom of the second inning against Louisville Southern, he was just hoping to make contact and get on base.

The pitch was in his zone, he swung, and he said he just started running. Then he heard the cheers and the senior catcher realized he had hit his first varsity homerun. The trot around the bases however was less a celebration of his accomplishment, and more of a tribute to his younger brother and teammate Joseph, who was killed just prior to the Bears' season in a car accident.

"I didn't really watch the ball go over, I was just running fast. Then I heard the crowd and realized it went over. At that moment, he was on my mind because I've never really hit a ball that hard. It made me think that Joe just might have helped me with a little more power tonight."

There was a slight smile on his face as he rounded the bases, and a group of happy teammates waiting for him at home plate. As he scored, he was met with high-fives, pats on the back and congratulations.

The homerun gave the Bears a 3-0 lead on their way to a 6-1 victory, but it lifted the spirits of everyone wearing blue Monday night. And also, the fans in the stands, which included his parents.

It's been a tough season. The Bears have struggled on the field at times, and losing a teammate can take a toll on a group of kids. Jacob's homerun seemed to erase a lot of the hurt that's piled up over the past couple of months.

Jacob said it has been difficult, but Joe, even in death, has brought his team closer together.

"We would not be the family we are now if it wasn't for Joe. Sure, we argue a little bit, but we all know even if this season's win-loss record is not the greatest—it's about the brotherhood. My brother brought us all closer together," he said.

He also credits his brother for Monday night's big hit. "When I got back to the dugout I said, 'Joe, that ball was for you and I know you were here to help.'"

"Even before the game, I knew there was something different about tonight. During school today, and during pregame warm-ups, he was just all I could think about all day. I guess he heard me talking to him and decided to show me that he could hear me."

Those who knew him said Joseph's life spoke for itself, but if there's any doubt that his spirit is no longer with those who knew and loved him, Jacob's got a homerun ball and a magical moment to prove them wrong.

Jacob plans to continue his baseball playing after high school. He'd attracted interest from schools in Kentucky, Indiana and West Virginia, but has decided to play for Midway University. Fortunately for Midway, Jacob will be carrying a piece of Joseph with him every time he steps onto the field.

∽

I love this! I remember standing looking at the picture of my phone and Coach Thad saying, " Well I guess Joe did show up here with us after all." It was amazing!

HE'S STILL WITH US

Our friend, Elizabeth Vannatta, shared this message on a Facebook post.

As today marks another year of the passing of sweet Joe, I want to bring this story to light again.

I was in the middle of volleyball practice when Belinda Sheeley walked in and asked to borrow me to take a picture of Jake's college baseball signing. As I was taking the picture, there was never a glare on the phone screen. It looked like a normal picture. But Joe shined down from the gates of the glorious Heaven to show he was there that day.

1 Thessalonians 4:13-14
Brothers and sisters, we do not want you to be uninformed about those who sleep in death, so that you do not grieve like the rest of mankind, who have no hope. For we believe that Jesus died and rose again, and so we believe that God will bring with Jesus those who have fallen asleep in him.

A VISIT WITH JOE

The following are several text messages between my friend, Dedra, and myself. She texted me this months after Joe's death, though the dream occurred just a week after he left. I never in a million years saw this coming.

> Hey Belinda! Hope you are doing okay. I have something to share with you. I hope you don't think I'm nuts.
>
> This week I had a trip to the ER. I will spare you the details, but it wasn't good. Anyway, the last thing I remember was telling Bud to call 911. For what seemed like days, but was only minutes, I was in a room full of light. I couldn't see much... then boom!
>
> I saw my Popaw who passed 20 years ago, I saw my brother Obie who passed 7 years ago. And I saw the old fella that I had been taking care of the past several months who just passed in February.

As we rejoiced and hugged, I saw someone in the distance. And I yelled "JOE!" When he turned, I saw the most beautiful face and smile. Then his face went blank, and he screamed "NO DEDRA!" I wept.

Joe yelled at me!!! He just kept saying No, No, No...

I ran for what felt like hours. When I reached him, I said, "Joe, what's wrong?" He said, in only a voice that could come from Joe, "You can't stay with me."

I cried.

He said, "You can't stay here, your family needs you there right now."

I was in the most beautiful place. On such a beautiful lake with your beautiful child. And he told me NO! We sat for what seemed like hours and talked, but it was probably only moments.

He said I had to go back.

Joe said, "I need you to tell my family to grieve because it's natural, but don't over-grieve. Love people like I did when I was there. That's how to keep me alive. Talk to and love people of all ages. Tell them about my life and my love of the Lord."

"But most of all take a message to my family. Tell Momma I see her cry, and that light shiver she gets is me... loving her neck and kissing her cheek. And tell her No one has to take me!"

(He said y'all would know what this means.)

(This means no one has to stop cooking supper and drive him to the lake, river, or pond to go fishing for five hours!)

"And Ethan, the best time of my life was the last several months just me and you talking late."

He said things changed and he got to spend extra time with Ethan. He didn't say what or why. Joe said, "Lose the guilt trip Big Bro... Nothing is your fault. I'm watching you... Try to keep your truck on the road! I was with you that day. I wasn't gonna let anything hurt you! I love you Big E!"

(Joe is talking about the car he wrecked in—it was Ethan's and he had been feeling guilty about letting Joe drive it that night.

And then six weeks after we lost Joe, Ethan had a wreck in a bad curve on the way to work and flipped his truck. He walked away without even a scratch, even though he wasn't wearing his seatbelt.

Dedra couldn't have known about it, because it happened while she was at the hospital.)

"And tell my Sissy she is a rock... She has taken care of Momma and everything she can so she's not overwhelmed. But, cry, grieve, Sissy. You are still strong, but let it out before it consumes your life. I love you and Waylon, Tristan, and Taylor, so take care of yourself too! I will be watching over your babies."

"And tell Elly when she wakes up at night giggling, I am tickling her. And when she feels sad, I am as close to her as I can get... I visit her the most at night to help her sleep. Tell her I lay beside her and rub her hair." Joe said y'all would know about that!!! Uncle Joe Joe will always protect her, always!

(Joseph would let Elly come lay in bed in the evening and he would tell her stories and rub her soft hair till she got sleepy.)

"Tell Jake I'm so proud of him! He's got so much living to do... Grieve for me... But don't let it consume your life. Live, laugh, and love!!! And when you need me, I am there with you. You can't see me, Jacob, but you'll know I'm near."

(I really believe Joe was with his brother the night he hit his home-run! Jake even said he felt something strengthen him for that hit.)

"And to my Daddy who cries just about every day. I see you... I ride with you a lot when you are working... I am your co-pilot and when you cry, I tap you on the shoulder and say, "Don't cry Daddy, I can go fishing, and no one has to take me now!""

Joe knew this was gonna happen to me before it happened, Belinda. He was waiting to get word back to you all that he's good and he said, "Even if I could be home, I wanna be here." I believe that he needed you all to know these things.

It was hard for me to do this, but I promised I would. I would never break a promise to any of our boys ever! I'm not crazy, this really happened! I sat with Joe on the bank of the biggest, clearest lake and talked to him for hours... When we were done, he kissed my cheek and hugged me and made me go back. I didn't come to myself until about 4pm.

This is not to upset you, I would never do that! I still dream of this every night. He doesn't want me to forget my promise, but I didn't know how you all would take this. You know me well enough to know this happened. I'm not crazy – this happened! I made up with my brother, and my Pop said he was proud of the wife and mother I am.

Dee, I don't think you're crazy at all. I will tell you that a couple of people don't think I'm grieving right, that I'm not crying enough about Joe. They think I'm a nut job lol. They're a little depressing to talk to. Luckily, I have lots of supportive friends who understand me.

But even before you shared any of this stuff with me, I have felt peace and comfort almost constantly. Even the night in the hospital when they told us Joe didn't make it – I knew he was dead, but that he was still with me – like I could feel him next to me. People have asked how I could smile at my son's funeral. I can't explain except to say that he's waiting for me, and yet he's with me. I feel it, I'm comforted by it and I trust in that.

Belinda, no one can tell you how to grieve. No one can judge your grief. That's your prerogative. How you grieve is your choice. Joe is fine – I am an eyewitness to that. He doesn't want your life to be full of grief and crying to consume you all.

Oh, believe me, I cry a little for myself every now and then because I miss him. But, it's hard to be sad that your kid is enjoying Heaven. I am completely and totally happy for him. I just gotta make sure everyone left here is gonna be with him one day. That's my job now!

It's hard to make sure everyone is going to Heaven. But it's worth the hassle. That place was beautiful! He will always be with you and the whole family. That's where his heart is. He just wanted to be with those he loves and now he can see y'all anytime. He said he has a bird's eye view!

Dee, you are amazing! I can't even imagine all you've experienced. I wish I could see what you saw! What a gift we have been given! How many people get messages from Heaven these days, Dee? This is like Biblical experiences that we are having here. I'm so overwhelmed right now. And I'm so glad it was you that God allowed to communicate with Joe!

Joe's headstone is beautiful and he thinks it's cool! I bought an angel to put on his grave, if you will let me. He's my angel and he saved me!

Have you told your family about your experience with Joe?

No ma'am. No one knows but you, not even my husband. He is having a hard time as it is with losing Joe. But, I hope we can share this because it shows hope, faith, love, compassion, happiness, and that's what Joe was all about.

Nope, this is yours. You share as you want. I will tell my family eventually. I'm still processing this, and still catching up. I am writing it all down and when I'm done, I will give you a copy to keep. He told me so many things. According to my time line, I was with Joe from 7ish to around 4 p.m. But he wouldn't let me stay.

He said he and Jesus were "tight" lol. And he taught Jesus his hand gestures so he wouldn't have to always say "hello." I about busted a gut lol.

I have confidence that what you say is real. Because there's too many private "Joe" things that I'm not sure you knew about lol. Dee, I'm sorry I haven't been here for you this past month. Please let me know when you need help! We love you. And Joe's right, your family needs you here. And your job here isn't done yet.

Thank you for sharing about Joe. It explains a lot of what's been happening here.

CANADIAN FISHING TRIP

After Joe's passing, many in our small town helped us out so much financially—we didn't have life insurance on Joe, so folks chipped in to do fundraisers to pay for funeral and burial costs as well as to help us pay bills while Eric was missing work.

One of the fundraisers was donated by a sweet couple who own Black Bear Lodge in Canada. They offered a rustic fishing trip at their place for two families of four and sold chances to win. The two families who won actually were friends of ours, and they absolutely insisted that we take the trip instead of them going. They both thought Joe would have wanted that for us.

We weren't too sure we wanted to be so far from home that summer, but we finally agreed we would go, and we took some of Joe's close friends along with us as well. What a blessing that trip was. It was healing, and therapeutic to say the least. It allowed us to be in God's nature, in His presence in a way we never had before. Joe would have loved it, but like Jacob pointed out, he was still there with us!

This is the letter we sent to the sweet people who sent us on that much needed trip.

Terri, David & Katie
Steve, Connie, Michael & Sarah

Just wanted to thank you again so much for giving us the opportunity to go on the Canada trip. I know I told you that this was the trip that Joe always wanted to take, so it felt a little strange at first going without him. But, thanks to you all, it was wonderful to go there and just be together in a way that would have made Joe very happy.

When you look at the pictures, the first thing we saw when we got on the lake was a full rainbow. It had rained (and hailed) on us for 8 miles coming down the logging road into the camp. But as soon as we pulled in, the rain stopped and this is what was over us the whole evening. It didn't leave until it got dark. We all decided that Joe was with us making sure we enjoyed our time together.

Thank you again for making the trip possible for us. And thank you for being so supportive during this tough patch we're going through.

We managed to find a lot of happiness, and a lot of healing, spending this time together. We definitely made some good memories together that we will treasure forever. And the guys said to tell you that the fishing was good too!

Love you all,
Belinda, Eric, Jacob, Ethan & Elly Sheeley

FISHING UPSTAIRS

This is a Facebook post from my son, Jacob, that was posted during the Canada trip that was given to us by a dear friend just after Joe's passing.

So, earlier today I was about to go fishing, and it was just me going out on the lake. And I realized the other seat in the boat was empty – and I was sitting at the dock just waiting… and waiting. I was waiting for about 20 minutes and then I realized I was waiting for someone who wasn't going to come with me today.

It's been about 4 months and it's still so hard to believe my brother wasn't here to enjoy Canada with me. He always wanted to come up here and fish, but I guess he's doing his own fishing upstairs.

And then he showed me he knew I was here. About 2 hours ago it was lightning and storming out and it looked like it would never lighten up, but it did. This is how he showed me

I miss you, Joe. Happy Fourth of July everyone.

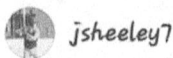 jsheeley7

THE HOLY SPIRIT

Have you ever felt the Holy Spirit cast a feeling over you that you just cannot explain? I was noticing this more and more after Joe passed away. The veil of comfort I felt was unmistakable and it could only be from the Lord. Same with the joy I felt when I was playing with my grandchildren. Only God could make me feel joy in light of what all we had been through.

BUT ONE EVENING I EXPERIENCED A NEW FEELING FOR THE FIRST TIME IN MY LIFE... A PANIC ATTACK.

Joseph and Jacob had started coon hunting when they were around fourteen and fifteen years old. It was something they both enjoyed and a huge part of the fun was training the dogs. They each managed to work and get enough money to buy their own dogs and they sure loved them. You could definitely see the special bond between them.

After Joe died, though, I think Jake wasn't as excited about going hunting without his brother. It was even a little hurtful to go out and mess with the dogs. I understood and my husband and I kind of took over the feeding and playtime at some point. Those dogs were hunters, but they were also attention hogs, and it was therapeutic for me to spend a lot of time with them.

One day I had asked Jacob to pick up dog food in Shelbyville while he was out. I didn't realize how low it had gotten. We got busy with life around the house and time got away from me and it was getting dark outside. I asked him where the dog food was and he told me he had forgotten it. I got so upset about it! Uncharacteristically upset over dog food! I fussed at him and told him to get to town and get some NOW! He felt so bad, so he went upstairs to grab his keys and headed out to leave.

As soon as I heard the front door close, though, I panicked! I looked at my husband and told him to stop Jacob! He couldn't go, I couldn't let him leave the driveway.

Eric ran to stop him, not knowing why. My heart was beating erratically and I couldn't catch my breath, I was running up the stairs trying to get to Jacob. He was still in the driveway when I came out. I was so relieved! Great, now everyone thought I was crazy and I couldn't explain why I didn't want him to go after I had just yelled at him to go!

My husband is a very kind, understanding man. He knew I must have a reason for the change of heart. And he could see the panicked look in my eyes. He thought I was just worried about Jake driving at night after Joe's wreck. So, he took the keys, and he drove to Shelbyville to pick up the dog food.

THIS TRIP SHOULD HAVE TAKEN ABOUT AN HOUR AT THE MOST.

After two hours, I was really getting worried. After three hours and no one answering my calls, I had a horrible feeling and I was pacing the house. Finally, I heard the truck pull in. I opened the door and found my sweet husband there in tears. He couldn't talk for a bit. I had to be patient and let him gather himself before he could explain.

There had been a wreck on the road ahead of him on his way back home. A single car with three teenagers had veered down off the road and flipped over. Eric and one other car were there behind them and called an ambulance. Two of the kids were fine, but one had been ejected from the car and lay on the embankment. Eric talked to him and held his hand, the lady from the other vehicle, who was a nurse, was checking his vitals. The ambulance took what seemed forever to get there.

Eric remembered how everyone was there for our boy, and he remembered how important it was to us knowing that Joe wasn't alone.

People were gathered around caring for him, assuring him, praying for him. Eric said he just couldn't leave this young man. Even when the EMT's were working on him, Eric kept talking to him... until he took his last breath.

When he shared his experience with me, I felt my heart fall. I was so sorry that Eric had to go through this so soon after losing Joe. But I was also grateful that it wasn't Jacob who experienced it. Eric pointed out that if I hadn't stopped Jacob from leaving the house, he may have been in the wreck as well. My panic attack wasn't an attack at all. Turns out it was the Lord trying to get my attention and give me a message. Thank you, Jesus!

A few days later, we were out front when a man pulled into our drive. He introduced himself as the step-father of the young man who had died. He said he knew about our boy and he wanted to thank Eric, he knew it must have been hard to go through that again.

These parents wanted to let us know how much it meant to them that their son wasn't alone in his last moments. One of the EMT's had told him and his wife that Eric refused to leave the boy and was praying over him even as they were working on him.

Sweet Eric wanted to make sure the boy was saved and going to Heaven. I pray he's there now with our Joe.

THE BEST GIFTS

November 29, 2017

Last month, a new photo customer of mine, unknowingly, gave me an amazing Christmas gift. I want to share it with you.

A lady, whom I've never met before, contacted me and asked me to restore an old photo for her. It was a smoke and water damaged picture of 3 little children sitting on the family car in their winter coats. Cute picture, but nothing remarkable – until she started telling the story of the picture.

— Belinda

You see, they were her children, back in the early 80's. The little boy on the left died when he was just five-years-old, just after this photo was taken. Then, just a year after his death, the family's home burned, including all their things, and all their pictures. Except this one—which was badly damaged. She held onto this damaged photograph for twenty-seven years, until she saw my Facebook post for my new restoration business.

I ADMIT, I WAS EXTREMELY ANXIOUS TO DO A GOOD JOB
FOR HER.

In light of all I have been through this past year, I felt determined to
give her something beautiful to hold in her hand - to look at and
remember—to keep her little boy's memory more alive—something
to share with her family.

While I had spent the past few months regretting I missed my
opportunity to take Joe's baseball pictures and senior portraits, I
began to let that sadness cloud my happier memories of Joe. I sometimes forgot to be thankful for all the memories he gave us and God
blessed us with.

I had been concentrating on what I was missing instead of
what I was given.

When I delivered her picture, she was so very happy. We both sat
there in the car in a grocery store parking lot crying. I shared with
her my inward struggle of the past few months and I thanked her
from the bottom of my heart for letting God use her to help me see
things from another perspective.

This lady, whom I had never met, was put in my path by God to
remind me of the blessings God *DID* give me. What a wonderful gift
for one mother to pass on to another.

I hope everyone can remember that the best gifts we can share with
each other don't necessarily come in a box or a bag, but from the
heart. Those are the gifts that last a lifetime. And they can be given
all year round.

JOY

December 2017

You're never too old to learn something new. I learned something important at church this Christmas season about joy.

Joy isn't a feeling—it's something you choose to find in all things. I think because of the way I was raised, and because of my faith in Jesus, I am able to find joy in life. My parents were really happy, positive people. And for that I'm thankful.

Finding the joy in things has lovely side-effects. It brings you peace and makes you happy. Joy is something you have to consciously choose each day.

Joy can be habit-forming, and it's contagious! People around you will notice that you're happy and positive. And when they ask, "Why are you in such a good mood?" you can say, "Because I chose the gift of joy from Jesus today."

Even when things don't go my way, even when the people I love aren't by my side, I choose to find joy in the treasured memories of them. And joy comforts me far more than sadness and grief.

The Christmas Angel Gabriel said to the shepherds, "I bring you tidings of great joy!" Even the news of Jesus' birth was filled with joy and the men were blessed to meet the King of Heaven and Earth. That's a wonderful Christmas gift to share with everyone!

I hope everyone I know has a wonderful, Joyous Christmas! (Fun fact: my middle name is Joy. I didn't fully appreciate that until last Sunday.)

— Belinda

LONG JOURNEY

I was talking to Mr. Sid and Mrs. Ann just after Joe died. They're a couple who live just down the road a little ways from us. They came to see how I was getting on. She said she still missed her son whom they lost almost twenty years ago. She told me that missing Joe will feel the same years from now. She cried while we were visiting. She said she still cries for her son a little every day.

Four years later and I'm just now starting to believe her.

I have many times gone days, even weeks, feeling at peace at where my kids are, and though I miss them terribly, I can exist in this life knowing they're waiting for me in Heaven. Then there are days—even now—that I get transported back to the day they both passed and I cry uncontrollably and can't seem to quit.

This is going to be a long journey requiring lots of prayer, which I knew. But sometimes it swallows me up and I just have to regroup again and keep moving forward.

So, I don't suppose grieving ever stops. It changes you. It changes as time goes on. But it doesn't stop. Does it get easier? Not sure there's an answer for that. It just gets more manageable if you let God help you through it. I really thought Ann was mistaken that day, that it would get better and I'd eventually not hurt so badly. But she knew...

— *Belinda*

FRIENDS FOR LIFE

This is a Facebook post by Bella Goodlett, a recipient of the Joseph Lee Taylor Sheeley "Friends for Life" Scholarship.

I had the wonderful honor of receiving the Joseph Lee Taylor Sheeley Scholarship tonight. I was flooded with all types of bittersweet emotion, and couldn't help but cry.

My year was not the greatest, but I always felt like Joe was beside me every step of the way. To remember Joe and all of the memories we had together, will forever be my favorite feeling. That smile & kind heart have left a permanent impact on my life. I had never met a boy who brought so much light with him no matter where he went.

When I see a neon orange sunset, a record bass on a hook, the fog on my deer stand window bright and early, or hear the song Dixieland Delight, I always think of you, Joe. Papaw Lewis would've loved to meet you, I'm glad you all can be together now.

Thank you, Joseph for being an angel and teaching me so much life in the short time we had together. Thank you, Joseph's family. You all are inspiring for your strength, and how you are using your hardships to Glorify

God's name. This has completed my somewhat incomplete senior year.
Joseph, I love you, Bub.

— *Bella Goodlett*

TAX RETURN

Never in my life had I ever seen a teenager so anxious to go to work! Truly, though, I suppose Joe had been working since he was eight years old or younger.

Around the house there were "extra" chores. Across the street there was the greenhouse where he would carry ladies' plants out to the car for them. He cut, topped, and hung tobacco in extreme heat for at least six summers.

BUT THE JOB HE WANTED MOST AT FOURTEEN WAS TO BE A BAGGER AT OUR SMALL-TOWN GROCERY STORE.

That still makes me laugh! He had me drive him there so many times to ask if he could work. Miss Ally told him he had to wait till he was sixteen—so frustrating! So, he waited. And on his sixteenth birthday he showed up at the store and said "I'm ready to work!" To my surprise, they actually did let him start.

He was a good worker—I knew he would be. Every job the boy did was 110 percent. He either caught a ride or walked to the store to work each day after school. I would make the drive to pick him up in the evening.

He bought a few things he had been wanting for baseball and hunting, but he pretty much saved most of his money. I was pretty impressed with his generosity.

He gave at church each Sunday, but he was especially interested one Sunday when one of our missionaries to Haiti came to talk to us. The missionary told about what they were doing in Haiti, the challenges they were facing and their goal of saving people's souls as well as building churches, providing medical care and more! Joe was so touched by the Holy Spirit. He asked Pastor Chad that very day if he could go on the next mission trip! Joseph now had a new reason to work hard and save those paychecks.

AND THEN CAME THE DREADED REALITY THAT IS TAX TIME.

A little depressing for us adults who have to pay on April 15. But, for a sixteen year old, it was pretty good news. When he went to the store owner, Miss Ally explained to him that he would get back all the taxes he had paid in over the past year. It wasn't but about $600. But to Joseph, it was A LOT!

Over the next few weeks, I could tell he was really thinking something over. He would usually come to me and talk things through, but this, this one he was trying to reason out for himself.

Finally, he came to his daddy and I asking what he should do when he got his tax check back. He had thought to pitch in and help buy the truck he had been wanting. But he really, really wanted to give his tax check to the missionary who had visited our church. He asked if that would be okay with us. Eric and I just looked at each other (and I was trying not to cry). His daddy told him it would be a pretty good thing to send that money to missions. When Joe knew we were on board with it, he was so relieved!

He went on and on about how they could use the money—food, building supplies, medicine, Bibles. I remember thinking that he may have overestimated slightly on what $600 could actually buy. He was so excited to donate it though, so I kept quiet. I actually prayed that it would be like the two fish and five loaves of bread and would multiply!

JOSEPH NEVER GOT HIS TAX CHECK IN THE MAIL.

His accident was March 4, and the check came in April. It broke my heart opening the envelope. I knew what was in it and I didn't want to look at it. But I finally shared it with the family and we all decided, of course, that we would send it to the church in Joe's name for his mission that he loved.

I found out later that because of Joe's excitement about the mission trip, Pastor Chad shared Joe's story and many other people gave as well. Perhaps God did multiply his gift like the loaves and fishes after all.

I still pray that Joe's selfless gift is blessing someone in Haiti.

LETTER TO JOSEPH

I wrote this letter to Joseph just after he was born. I wanted to jot it down while it was fresh in my memory so I didn't forget any of it. Which is funny now, because I haven't forgotten ANY of it after all these years! It *was* a little traumatic I guess.

Dear Little Joseph,

This letter is being written to you while you are still a tiny little baby. Someday when you are grown and have children of your own, it might be fun to share this with them! This is the story of how you arrived in this world. You weren't born in a hospital like your sister and brothers. You had to be different!

Let me back up a bit, though. Several weeks before you were born, I started having false labor pains late in the evenings. Sometimes it was awful, sometimes it was mild. The doctor assured me that it was normal and I was to take it easy and put my feet up more. Monday, the day before you were born I had a check-up with my doctor. I told her I thought I was close to delivering, but she assured me I had at least four to six more weeks.

So, Monday night I had grocery shopping to do. I went by myself to Kroger, the one in Shelbyville. About halfway through the store, I noticed I was having "false" labor pains again. I got home and Dad and Ethan helped put away the groceries and I went to bed to try to sleep off the discomfort.

Well, about 12:30 a.m. I woke up in a bit of pain. I didn't say anything to your Dad. I just figured it wasn't the real thing yet anyway, so why wake him? At about 1:30 a.m. I called the doctor's answering service. The doctor called me back and said I may need to be checked out at the hospital. But, I didn't want another false run to the hospital where they send you back home right after you walk in the door. So, I did the only thing I thought would help. I took a shower. I heard that it relaxes your body and if you're in false labor it will stop. I made a discovery, however. If you're in real labor it speeds things up!

I woke your Daddy around 3 a.m. and told him it was time – NOW! Well, he got up out of the bed so fast that he made himself sick. Yes, I was ready to leave and I had to wait for him to finish in the bathroom. Poor thing. I felt so sorry for him – in between the contractions, that is.

Well, in the meantime, I had called Carol, our neighbor to come and sit with Ethan and Jacob while we went to the hospital. We wound up taking her car, because the way the hospital garage is set up, we couldn't get our big conversion van inside. On the way to the car, I had a contraction so strong it nearly knocked me down. I held on to Carol through it and told your Daddy he better take me to the Shelbyville Hospital instead of Norton's because I didn't think we would make it. He assured me that we could make Norton Kosair's just as fast. I sent him back in to get a big blanket for the seat of the car just in case my water broke on the way. So off we went in Carol's Dodge Dynasty (with the plush velour seats).

Now normally, your Daddy's a good, safe driver. But at 4:30 a.m. on an empty, dark road he really can fly pretty fast. And I was coaching him (yelling at him) to drive faster and faster. I kept mentioning that I wasn't going to make it to the hospital. He kept saying we would. We made it in and out of Taylorsville in record time. We made it all the way down 155 and Taylorsville Road to the Snyder Freeway. We even made it to I-64 and Blankenbaker Road. But that's all the farther we made it. At one point he was going to take us to Suburban Hospital. But we didn't even make it that far.

Yes, you were born in a moving car at 90 miles an hour on I-64 at Blankenbaker. Daddy didn't have time to stop and help me because you came so fast. Oh, he wanted to. He did slow down and ease off the road up the ramp, but by that time I was already holding you unwrapping the cord from your little legs and looking into your eyes. Daddy asked if we were okay, and I said I thought so. Daddy turned the heat up in the car to keep you warm, and I covered you and me up with the big blanket he had brought for us. I did my best to clean the fluid out of your nose and mouth. I made you sneeze somehow, and you cleaned out your own nose.

I remember praying you would be okay. And I really think God gave your Daddy and I the calm patience to deal with the situation. We didn't get upset or anything. We just did what we had to do and actually had a cheerful attitude about it all. We even laughed about what everyone would think about your arrival.

We arrived at the hospital about ten minutes after your birth due to the lightning speed of your Dad's driving. Dad had been on the cell phone in the car with the Doctor earlier and he and the nurses were ready to meet us at the door when we arrived at Norton's. The delivery room nurses came to the car with warm blankets and medical tools. They put drops in your pretty blue eyes, clamped and cut the cord, and wrapped you in a big warm blanket and rushed you in to the exam room. I got myself into the wheelchair and they took me to the recovery room.

The nurses and the doctor were a little surprised at how level headed and calm your Dad and I had been through the whole ordeal. They were especially surprised that we were laughing and making jokes with them about it. I told the doctor he better not even think about charging me for the delivery!

Well, a little time went by, and my exam was over. I was really wanting them to bring you back in to me. But, when the nurse went through the hall with you and said, "He'll have to see you later, Mom and Dad," I figured something had gone wrong. They assured us that you just had a little fluid in your lungs, and since you were about a month early, it was causing some complications. They had to get the fluid out of your lungs and you were promptly sent to Neonatal Intensive Care at Kosair and hooked up to a ventilator tube.

They took such good care of you there. All the nurses in your wing loved working with you because, at 6 pounds, you were the biggest baby they had in there at the time and you were cuddly. It was about 3 days, though, before the tube came out and I got to hold you again. Daddy was nervous to hold you because you were so tiny and still hooked up to so many wires. They had to send me home from the hospital without you and it nearly broke my heart. But, I knew you were getting the best possible care.

Finally, after 5 long weeks, we got to bring you home to your sister and your brothers! No one was ever so happy to have a new baby at home. You were spoiled quite thoroughly since Tori was 15 and Ethan was 9. You never got left alone unless they were at school. But it was a good kind of spoiled, because you were a delightful, happy baby, like your brother, Jacob. I wish all the babies in world felt as loved and cherished as mine.

— Momma

MARRIAGE

Someone told me just after Joe died that it was unfortunately common for couples who lose a child to get divorced. Not sure why they were sharing this with me—seemed a little bit of a downer. It never crossed my mind that could happen, and it sounded absolutely absurd!

Perhaps they were unfamiliar with the trials my husband and I have already come through. Or perhaps they didn't have the depth of devotion that Eric and I have for one another. Whatever the case, if losing a child doesn't make a married couple cling together and pray together and lean on Jesus together, then I suppose it could end in divorce.

But wouldn't that be unfortunate. To not be there for each other.

I wonder perhaps if that happens to couples who are not Christians? I can't speak for anyone other than myself and my husband, but for us, we both clung to each other more than ever before!

Emotionally and mostly spiritually. We shared together more about our faith at that time than ever before! We agreed that God would see us through this horrible loss. We looked at how, in the Bible, Job suffered through harder situations than this, multiple times, and God always saw him through. We knew He would see us through, as well.

God makes many promises in the Bible. All of them are true. But my favorite is that He will never leave us, we can always call upon Him and He will be with us. I love that so much.

ONE YEAR

March 16, 2018

My Sweet Joe,

It's been over a year since you left us to go home to Heaven. I'm sorry I missed posting this on March 4th, but I was a little busy with your sister, whom I'm certain you now have in your arms.

We miss you both something awful, but I wouldn't wish you back here — because I know that where you are is amazing. And we look forward to coming there to Heaven with you one day when God is done using us here.

Love you, Joe!!! Really do miss that big ole smile! Hug Sissy for me!

— Momma

HAPPY BIRTHDAY

May 16, 2018

Happy Birthday Joe Joe!

Sure have been missing you a bunch. I guess that will never change. I think of you every day – and you always bring a smile to my face, just like when you were here.

I'm so thankful for the fun our family had together. Whether we were fishing together, or playing "name that tune" at the kitchen table while we ate supper – seems like we all spent our time trying to make each other laugh.

I wouldn't change a thing about our family. I love you boy! We'll see you soon…

— Momma

PRAYERS FOR BLAKE

February 8, 2019

A family we know in the next county over just lost their son in a horrible car wreck. I feel their pain to the depths of my soul. This is my prayer for them.

I hope that everyone will join me in praying for Blake's whole family. A piece of their life and heart now lives in Heaven. And while that is a comfort, that empty chair at the table, and that empty bedroom, and those empty baseball cleats leave you feeling... empty.

My prayer is that God shows them ways to help fill in those empty spots with the sweetest memories of Blake. Though his life, like my children, was over way too soon for us here, we need to remember to praise God and thank Him for the gift of every single moment we got to spend with them.

God, please use us to help this family through their loss.

— Belinda

FOUR YEARS

March 4, 2021

Missing you for 4 years.

Four years ago a lot of lives changed forever. You left an empty spot at our table, at school, at church, and in lots of hearts. But we're all so much better for having you in our lives even though it was for a short time. God was good to give you to us. And He was good to bring you to Heaven. We still miss your sweet face, your beautiful smile and your big old country accent so much! But we know we will see you again!

Love you Joe Joe.

Miss you so very much my little country boy!

— Belinda

POEM

Joseph wrote this little poem for his friend Lukas when his granddad passed away in 2016. He gave this to him when they were hunting one night and it meant a lot to Lukas. One year later, we lost Joe and Lukas was sweet enough to share it with me. He even showed me the spot where Joe gave it to him. This is **so** Joseph!

"When I die, don't cry,
Bury me with a smile,
And if you think for awhile,
It's never goodbye – Just see ya later!"

—JOSEPH SHEELEY

TORI

The following pages highlight my Friday morning phone conversation with my daughter, Victoria, just before our lives turned upside-down once again. This was on February 23, 2018.

11 A.M.

I called Tori at the hospital and asked how she was doing and let her know we were heading down to the hospital to see her.

To our surprise, they told her they were discharging her. Her father had spent the night at the hospital with her, so he offered to drive her back to her home.

I asked if her fever was down, and she said no. She said, "They're letting me go. I still feel strange, but I guess I must be okay because they're discharging me." I said, "Do you want me to come down and get you? I can be there in 45." She said, "No, dad's still here, the nurse caught him in the hall and he's gonna take me."

APPROXIMATELY 5 P.M., MONDAY AFTERNOON PHONE CONVERSATION

Tori called me as I was headed from Louisville to Mt. Eden on I-64. She said, "Mom, I still feel so bad—something's still wrong with me. I've been sitting still trying to rest, but my heart is racing like I just ran a marathon." I said, "They shouldn't have sent you home with a fever. You need to get back to the hospital NOW. Do you want me to turn around and meet you at Jewish?" She said, "No Mom, I don't think I'll make it to Jewish from here. I'm just gonna have Josh run me to the ER in Bardstown, just meet me at Flaget." I said, "I'm gonna run by the house and get Eric and we will be out there as fast as we can. What about the baby?" She said, "Josh will bring the baby back to the house, they'll just drop me off if you're gonna come out."

So, I hurried home, got my husband, and headed to Flaget. By the time we got there, they had her on meds to slow her heart rate down —but they said she was still not stable and needed to get transported to Jewish ASAP. She was freezing cold—her hands and feet were miserably cold to touch. My husband kept going to the hall to get warm towels and stood at the foot of her bed wrapping her feet and rubbing them trying to warm her up while I held her hands.

Finally, they got her an ambulance to take her to Jewish around 11:30 p.m. She asked me to go to her house to sit with the baby overnight so that Josh could come down to the hospital and stay with her overnight. We hugged her and kissed her, told her we loved her and we would take care of the baby. Then they put her in the ambulance. I tried to hide out of her sight because I was starting to cry—I couldn't hold it together anymore. But, she saw me and said, "You know I can see you crying, right? I'll see you in the morning." Those were the last words I ever heard my daughter say.

MONDAY 12 A.M.

The ambulance pulled away with my daughter and Eric and I went to take care of the baby. Josh went to stay with Tori at the hospital. I never dreamed in a million years that would be the last time I ever saw her pretty eyes looking at me—smiling at me.

MONDAY 8 A.M.

Josh called to tell me that the doctor had been in at 7 a.m. and had recommended that Tori be put into an induced coma so that they could work on her heart. I still had the baby and couldn't get to my child. My oldest son, Ethan, came and stayed with Baby Taylor so that I could go to the hospital. On the way there, it dawned on me that no doctor had seen her when she was admitted at midnight. She was put in a room and no doctor saw her or helped her until 7 a.m. I'm still wondering how that makes any sense? No one asked me to sign off on any paperwork for any of her procedures at that point.

HUG SOMEONE THAT MATTERS TO YOU

February 24, 2018

Just wanted to take a minute to let everyone know what has been happening before it gets thru the grape vine. Friday morning I had a heart attack. I'm going to be ok.

I'm in good hands with my family and wonderful doctors. I've been in the hospital since Friday afternoon, but should (fingers crossed) be coming home tomorrow. My body and mind are both exhausted. So, you'll have to excuse me if I don't answer or see every message.

Love you all! Go hug someone that matters to you!

— Tori

Go Hug Someone That Matters to You! – Victoria Whitehouse

That's one of the last posts my daughter put on her Facebook page. I've always wondered if she knew somewhere in her mind that she wouldn't be hugging us ever again.

IT'S SUCH A SIMPLE LITTLE THING TO DO, ISN'T IT? TO HUG SOMEONE?

Why then, do we drop our kids at school with no hug? Why do we leave the grandparents home without a hug? Or the parents? Or the dear friends?

I get that some people aren't huggers. But at the funeral, where you wished that you had one more chance to see your loved one, I bet hugging would be the first thing you'd want to do to them.

Our family, for the most part, never leaves anywhere without a hug and a very sincere "I love you." That makes my heart so happy. Because I had few regrets in this area when both of my children died. Totally different circumstances, but a lifetime of hugs and "I love you's" makes me able to have good memories now that they are gone. I tell people often, when I get to Heaven, I am running to hug Jesus first... but then I am going to hug my children!

Tori posted this to encourage her friends to show their families the affection and love she enjoyed with her children and her family. In this day of uncertainty and confusion in which we live, it's so reassuring to a child, a teenager, or an adult, to know that someone loves them enough to share a hug and a smile, and their unconditional love.

And it's so easy... just a hug means so much.

FACEBOOK POST UPDATES

The following are Facebook posts that I did to update folks about my daughter. As we stayed in the hospital over the next three and a half weeks, I tried to keep folks updated on her situation.

FEBRUARY 27, 2018

Today is Waylon's 11th birthday. His Momma can't be at the party she planned for him. I am here at the hospital while everyone else tries to give him a "normal" birthday party. I am so thankful for Matthew and his wife, Erin, Waylon's and Tristan's step-mom. She is a blessing from Heaven. The boys will need her strength and her love. She helped them make get-well cards for their Momma at the party and had them delivered to the hospital to hang on the wall in her room, just in case she opened her eyes today.

— Belinda

FEBRUARY 28, 2018

So, today, I had to watch as my 32 year-old sweet daughter lay in the

Cardiac Care Unit in the fight of her life. Or maybe I should say the fight for her life. My perfectly healthy Victoria has been having a heart attack since Friday afternoon... today is Tuesday.

After 2 heart caths and an ineffective pump surgically placed in her leg, the cardiologist now has her in a medically induced coma to rest her heart – her heart that has been operating at only 20% of its required function. A bypass machine is moving the blood through her body for her. An oxygen machine is breathing for her. About 50 monitors are displaying activity and levels that I have no idea what all they mean. And my girl is laying lifeless amongst it all. In two to three days, if she can successfully be weaned off the machine and her heart works properly on its own, she will be on the long road to recovery. If this pump does not work, there are only 2 options left – one other type of pump inserted in her heart – or a heart transplant.

But God is good, and I know that He works through medicine as well as His own Divine Healing. Please pray with me for Victoria that her heart responds to the rest, the treatment and the medication from the doctors, as well as from God's healing hand.

— Belinda

MARCH 2, 2018

I try to be strong. For Tori, for my husband, my boys and my grandbabies. I believe my God has this in His control – I really do. But when I get tired, in mind or in body, Satan attacks. And it's then that I am carried by the love and prayers of my family and friends – by people who are my family by choice – even by some people who are praying whom I haven't even met. It is by your prayers to God, in the name of Jesus that I gather more strength to carry on.

If anyone doesn't believe in the power of prayer in the name of Jesus...step into my shoes and get a firsthand look. It's humbling, it's comforting, and it's amazing to feel so secure in God's hands and within the arms of all the people loving on us.

I don't know God's will for Victoria. But I know God hears our earnest pleas for her healing. So, my prayer is simply this…

Thank you, Lord for the daughter You've given me. Thank you for the strong, wonderful mother she has become. Thank you for making her a kind, loving woman. Please heal her heart completely. Make her heart, her kidneys, and her liver whole again. Repair any damage to her body so she can come back to us. As her Momma, I ask You to work a miracle in this hospital that will rock these halls and make these doctors marvel at your power. It's a tall request, but You're my God and I know only You can help her now. I give my girl into Your hands in the name of Your sweet Son Jesus. Amen

— Belinda

MARCH 3, 2018

Update: The Rhino Virus, i.e., the common cold

REALLY?!! That's the virus settled in our girl's heart? How does this happen? It attacked her heart and made it swell, and then stopped working. And a different virus, merexella, also settled into the entrance to her lungs.

The doctors won't be measuring her heart activity for a few more days. Just letting it rest and continue to heal. However, I did want to share that her skin color now looks beautiful (not pale and yellow) and her blood pressure has stabilized enough that they tweaked back the kidney dialysis even more. Her liver functions continue to improve – slowly, but steadily. And big news – they have just started giving her nutrition through her feeding tube. Praise God for every tiny improvement. Around midnight, the nurse dialed back the sedative to do the neuro check. She asked Tori to open her eyes and squeeze her fingers – and SHE DID IT!!! To me that was like winning gold at the Olympics, or better! Very exciting!

I just spent time with Tori. Is it strange that amidst all the tubes and machinery hooked up to my baby, that I can still see the beauty that is my girl? I look at her pretty face, and her strength and sweet spirit nearly radiate from her. I feel like I can hear her voice in my mind and I know exactly what she's thinking. I know how she will respond to certain comments people make in the room around her. I don't know if it's a "mom thing" that we are in tune with each other, or perhaps we are just so similar in personality. Thanks to everyone who continues to lift up our whole family in prayer – especially Victoria, Waylon, Tristan and Baby Taylor. I believe in my heart she will, with God's help, overcome this.

— *Belinda*

MARCH 5, 2018

Just wanted to share some random pics of Tori with you. Some of you don't know my girl. She's a devoted daughter, and an amazing Momma. She is family oriented and a fierce friend to have in your corner. She's vibrant, tough, sweet, soft-hearted, and giving to a fault. She's a child of God and a follower of Jesus. And she is my very beautiful special girl.

— *Belinda*

MARCH 5, 2018

Tests this morning showed no large clots – surgery started at 1:30 p.m. – hopefully done in 8 hours. Tell your family members and friends today how much you love them. And give them a hug – and really mean it. Thanks for the continued stream of prayers. Will let you know more when we get news. And now we wait…

MARCH 5, 2018

Ready for the best update? Surgery was a success! The LVAD pump was inserted in the left side of Tori's heart and is causing her heart to move the blood through her body so much better! The doctor did not feel it necessary at this time to insert an additional pump in the right side of the heart. We are going to see if it will "get with the program" on its own. So your job is to pray about that!!! She is certainly better – but not out of the woods. Your continued prayers are worth everything to our family. Thank you for hanging in there with us and loving on us – we sure love every one of y'all!

MARCH 6, 2018

Today, our goal for Tori is to just take it easy and keep her levels all stable and even. She has a foreign object in her heart (a new pump) and her body will probably take awhile to acclimate. I'm just so relieved and amazed and thankful she's still with us. I just stand and stare at her all night and hold her hand and sing to her and talk to her. She still looks like she has good skin color. Just got to get her used to this pump and pray it moves enough blood to the extremities. She is still on the ECMO life support machine to support the right side of her heart. They are hoping that the right ventricle will begin pumping on its own. Her chances are looking better than before, so that's definitely an answer to prayer. But we still have such a long way to go. But my girl is strong and my God is great. This can happen – and we covet your prayers so much. It's not only getting Tori through, but us as well. Thanks to everyone helping us through prayer, meals, visits – just everything! We have the best support group EVER!

MARCH 7, 2018

So... at 5:30 a.m. our nurse came out and woke us up (which doesn't ever happen for good reasons). Tori's oxygen has decreased significantly throughout the night and her levels are now at a detrimental level. They are moving her central line out of the right side of her neck and are running a new ECMO line into the right side of her neck to provide her more oxygen into her lungs. The surgeon will perform the procedure in her room around 7 a.m. Without the added oxygen, her other organs will begin to deteriorate again. So please pray for oxygen! And continued healing of the liver! And kidneys! And continued oxygen to the brain! And healing of the heart! WOW – I know that's a LOT! Good thing Jesus – the greatest healer EVER is on our team!

They ran the new central line of the ECMO through her neck to get her oxygen levels up where they need to be. The downside of that is that they have had to put her on complete paralysis to allow her to heal with absolutely no chance of movement from her. The upside is that her oxygen rates are already improving. These are a lot of ups and downs, and yes, I was a basket case for a bit. But I believe God has gotten her this far, and will continue to make her heal. Thank you for hanging in there with us. I feel like we have this huge "family" of folks rooting for us – and that means the world to us that y'all love our Tori so much.

MARCH 8, 2018

Update: Tori had a good night!!! Numbers are up where they're supposed to be and they are actually getting ready to do a surgical procedure to remove the ECMO line that's supporting the right side of her heart to see if it can work on its own. Very excited to see if it works – Huge Step! Just pray and ask Jesus for good right-heart action after this line comes out. My sweet pretty girl is gonna win this fight! Thank you all for helping her!

MARCH 8, 2018

Things I think about in the middle of the night:
My family is so blessed to live in a community where people still genuinely love and take care of one another as God tells us to do. At our most difficult times, we have felt the support, compassion and love pouring out to us from friends, church family – some people who don't even know us that well, who just know our circumstances. And I am always so impressed with the younger folks that keep sending love our way. You just don't realize the strength you give us when you visit or pray with us. With everything bad going on in the world right now, take heart. There are more Godly, wonderful folks out there than you realize. And it's an awesome gift to know they've got our backs right now. We appreciate and love y'all!

MARCH 11, 2018

Update: I've been with Tori tonight trying to get responses out of her – she's nodding a little when I talk to her and doing that squinch eyebrow thing. Also got a little hand squeeze action too – from both hands! And big news of the night from the nurse – she can finally find a pulse in both feet and both hands!!

This is a HUGE change from this morning. I spent from 6-9:30 a.m. thinking I was telling her goodbye. Our nurse was emotional and crying with me and it seemed like it was going to be over. At that time our options all looked dismal. But somehow, through prayer and relinquishing control to God, He turned things around for us! Praise!!

This rollercoaster ride is rough! Big thanks to every single person for every single prayer and every word of encouragement. Your support continues to lift us and amaze us. My girl is going to have an incredible testimony when she gets better.

MARCH 12, 2018

Update on Tori: At 9:30 a.m. we meet with doctors to discuss some complications that Tori is experiencing and how to resolve them and what our options may be. Please pray with me for God to reveal His wisdom to us that we may make the best decisions for Tori this morning.

Thanks to everyone following her progress and praying for Tori and our family. We believe in a great God. He has been so good to wrap His arms around our family by giving us His comfort through friends like you. Your comments touch our hearts every single day and I read them to my girl as she lays here sleeping. I pray for her body and her spirit to stay strong.

Update on Tori: 11:12 a.m. - We met with her doctor this morning to discuss where she is at in her process to recovery. Last night, they did find that she has a blood clot in the LVAD pump. This is very scary to hear, but the doctor did inform us that this is not uncommon and there is a plan in place to resolve the issue. We just pray for the first option that a little additional blood thinners will dissolve it and we move on. The doctor seemed to be in more uplifting spirits and we talked about how her condition just takes time and although it seems impossible, we have to be patient and continue our prayers and keep our hopes and spirits high. So please continue to pray with us.

MARCH 13, 2018

Update: Sorry to be so long filling you in, but we have been living minute to minute with information changing so fast we can barely keep up ourselves. We've been back and forth trying to get these blood clots dissolved out of her new LVAD pump. Thought they were gone – then they are back. Talk about a rollercoaster ride – complete with lots of butterflies in my stomach!

Right now we are just praying for God's will – her lungs are taking a hit right now, so we really need those lungs and her right heart to heal significantly in the next week so the doctors can move her to the next level.

Our family is so fortunate to have an army of friends praying for our Tori, as well as the rest of us. We treasure each prayer you pray and we simply ask that God hold and comfort Tori through this trial. Love y'all more than we can say!!!

MARCH 14, 2018

Tonight our entire family needs prayer — especially Tori. If you've ever asked God for a true miracle, please ask for one tonight.

Tori needs her miracle really soon. Because we need her… her babies need her.

She's been my best friend for 32 years.

Momma's still rootin' for you girl!

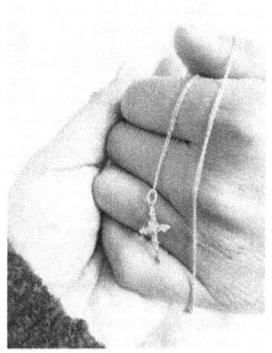

MARCH 16, 2018

7:53 a.m. — Still at the hospital… it won't be long now. Please pray for God to give me strength and grace to accept His will. Another piece of my heart is going to Heaven in a short while.

Everyone keeps asking if they can help us or do anything for us. Y'all have been the best support group ever. But I finally thought of something you all can do — if every single Facebook friend told just one person about Jesus today, what a cool way to usher my baby girl into Heaven today!

1:13 p.m. - As I sit here alone talking to Tori, I have made my peace with our situation. I don't understand why God wants my babies, perhaps because they are so good and sweet. Whatever His reasons, though, I have come to one conclusion at least. If only one person comes to know Jesus in their heart from our experiences with Tori or Joe, it would have been worth everything we've been through to see just one more friend find salvation.

MARCH 16, 2018

We took Tori off of life support today at 3:49 p.m.

Last Update: Tori is with Jesus now. She went so peacefully and with no pain. And she listened to recordings of her children's voices till her very last breath and was surrounded by all her family.

Tori died on March 16, 2018 – a year and 12 days after Joseph died

John 3:16 was her favorite Bible verse

Hmmmm…

March 16th (3/16)... It's John 3:16 Day!

Please consider posting John 3:16 on your FB page:

"For God so loved the world, that He gave His only begotten Son, that whosoever believeth in Him, should not perish, but have everlasting life."

WHOSOEVER DAY!!!!!!!!!

I'm so glad to be a WHOSOEVER.

MOMMA'S IN HEAVEN

My daughter had been on life support for several weeks. The doctors had tried everything they could to make her better. It just was not meant to be. God had other plans.

So, I had to sign the paperwork to remove her from the machines that were keeping her heart beating. I still am not sure how I even held the pen to sign my name, my hands were shaking so badly.

MY PASTOR AND MUCH OF TORI'S FAMILY GATHERED AROUND HER BED IN THE ICU TO BE WITH HER WHEN SHE TOOK HER LAST BREATH.

The doctor explained to us that sometimes when they remove the breathing tube, it seems like the patient struggles for the next breath and it can be very upsetting to the family. I looked the doctor in the eye and told her to go ahead. I prayed that there wouldn't be a bad reaction like that.

I didn't realize how accustomed I had gotten to all the noise from the machines keeping Tori alive. The beeping, the air moving through the hose to her lungs, the inflation of the leg wraps to avoid blood clots, the heart machine moving the blood through her heart and her body. It was suddenly quiet. I prayed she would be peaceful. And she was. She just let out a soft sigh of her last breath and was gone.

How could she look so beautiful and be gone – just like that?

The doctors and nurses left us so we could say our goodbyes. When it was my turn, I just said, "It's never goodbye, but I'll see ya later, my girl." Those were her brother, Joe's words in a poem to a friend who had lost his grandfather.

It was 3:49 p.m.

I hadn't left the hospital in so long, I didn't feel like I was ready to leave. But our friends came to bring us home, so off we went. I didn't feel like talking just yet. So, Eric made a phone call so that Tori's children would know their Momma was gone.

Matthew, Tori's ex-husband, answered and when Eric told him the news, he was a little taken aback at Matthew's response. Matthew already knew Tori was gone. We asked who called and told him. He said, "No one called. Tristan told me." Okay, we were all getting chills now.

Tristan, who was six at the time, had been in his room playing with his dinosaurs. Matthew said he came out to the living room and told him that his Momma was in Heaven. Matthew picked him up and hugged him and said, "Honey, how do you know your Momma's in Heaven?" Tristan looked him in the eye and said, "Because Daddy, Joe was in my room with me and told me so."

Chills again.

I love when God sends a guardian angel to take care of my grand-babies. God loves His children so much. I love that God reveals

Himself to children. I love that God uses children to teach us grownups lessons. Thank you, Jesus!

FRIENDS

I am fortunate to be able to say that I have a wonderful group of very close, special girlfriends. We actually call ourselves "Family."

I am proud to call these ladies my friends. Not only because they are kind hearted, good people, but because we have a common bond among us—we love each other in the Lord. And that makes us able to love each other on a whole other level. These ladies always have my back unconditionally. And no matter what I'm going through, they're on my side and in my corner. The same is true for Eric and the husbands in our "Family."

They have been in an emergency room in the middle of the night to pick up the pieces of my heart as my son died. And they have been in the NVICU waiting room for countless hours bringing me meals and keeping me company. Understanding why I refused to leave my daughter's side in the hospital for over three weeks *and* backing me up on it. And then waiting and just being there for me as my daughter was taken off of life support and left this world.

Tonight, at a gathering for my family, my friends were there for me again, and as I mingled with a huge crowd of people (which is very difficult for me), anytime I began to get overwhelmed and a little panicked, I had only to look up and catch the eye of one of these ladies—my dearest friends—and I was okay to keep moving on.

They make me stronger and remind me I am not alone.

They remind me that I can do more than I think I can. They are encouraging and positive and loyal, and that is hard to find these days. God has blessed me with good friends. And I am so thankful to have them in my life.

I pray that any who read this are inspired to *BE* that gift of a dear friend to someone else. Someone whom you may not even realize needs you. Pray and ask God to place someone in your path who needs a friend. Be there for each other. What an amazing gift for everyone!

HOME NOW

Well, here I am again, writing last words for one of my children. My oldest child, my only girl, my best friend. I wrote Joe's eulogy, but I wasn't able to speak it. Pastor Chad read it for me. But this one, I intend to deliver myself. And God will hold me up while I do it. It's important in my mind that I do it because I am so very proud of the woman and the mother my daughter grew to be.

— Belinda

Here is Tori's eulogy that I wrote and spoke at her funeral.

I lost another piece of my heart on March 16. Jesus came and took my sweet Tori to Heaven. She was so strong and fought as hard and as long as she could.

While we didn't get the miracle we hoped for, we did get a special gift. We got over 4,000 people via Facebook—family members, friends, and even strangers praying to the Lord literally around the clock and around the world. Praying together for Tori brought us all closer to each other and closer to Jesus.

Tori used to laugh and tell me all the time that I was psychic. Whenever she would call me, I would say "I was just thinking about you!" She thought I was Jedi-mind-tricking her to call me. Fact is, I just would ride down the road thinking about her and the boys a lot. I've caught myself several times the past few days picking up the phone to tell her something. I'll miss having my best girl to talk to.

I'm so glad that her sparkling eyes and contagious smile will still be looking back at us through the faces of her children. Each time we look into the faces of Waylon, Tristan, and Taylor, we will see Tori shining in their smiling eyes. What a blessing they are to our family.

Tori's fun-loving, free spirit was contagious. She was practical, smart, hilarious, witty, happy and just a little OCD. And she was the best Momma ever! She used to think she needed to work outside the home to be able to help provide for the family. But she came to realize God wanted her right where she was—at home raising her babies. What a wonderful gift God gave to those children. They were the light of her life—and she was the light of theirs. Her motherly instincts literally saved her children's lives more than a few times. She loved as a mother should and was a fierce protector like a mama bear.

She was beautiful outside and inside and was a champion for those in need. When Joe died, many of his friends struggled so much—and they would call or message Tori, often late at night when it was hard to sleep from the pain of their loss. And she always had time for them. She always put others' needs before her own. Tori never really had her own personal closure over losing Joe—so it eases my heart to know they are together once again.

Many folks, myself included, have asked "Why God?" In Tori's hospital room, I was so devastated and I cried out loud and asked my grandmother, "Why does God keep taking my babies?!" As soon as the question was out of my mouth, the answer flooded my head. My children BELONG to God. They were never really mine to keep—only to love and raise them up and teach them how to love God and others. And then be willing to give them back to Him. God wasn't selfish with His own Son, Jesus, so I can't be selfish with my children either. Yes, I would like to have kept Tori and Joe much longer, but who better to bring into Heaven and reward them for the *sweet hearts than Tori and Joe? I'm so happy for my children, to know right where they are, waiting for the rest of us to join them one day soon.*

All of us here have a job now. Our job is to make sure ALL our family and friends make it to Heaven as well. As parents, grandparents, and even good friends, make sure that everyone you love is saved. Tori and Joe believed in Jesus. He lived in them. That is what makes is loss bearable. That is where I draw comfort. And that is faith.

Satan wants us to feel cut off and alone in our grief. It's easier for him to work on us if we're feeling down and lonely. So, let's surround ourselves with faithful believers who can help us feel the hope that God offers to us.

Now is the time to believe what we believe in. That is what will get us all through this together.

My daughter's last texts to my mother and sister were very poignant…

"Headed home"
"I'm home now"

My girl really is home now.

LIVE LIKE TORI

This is a Facebook Post for Tori from one of Joseph's friends, Logan.

We all come together in this little town, but most importantly we all have faith in the good Lord. This family has been through so much it's crazy to the point most people (or families) would lose faith. But not this family or group of friends. God has a great big smile on His face and Jesus and Joe are smiling right now at these two strong women, Belinda Sheeley and Victoria Whitehouse. They couldn't be more proud of you two. They will both welcome Tori with open arms, and Tori and Joe will be the best two guardian angels you could have for you and your family.

Most people wanna ask why, but not once has anyone lost their faith, but only kept praying harder and harder. We love you so much and your family has a great group of friends and we will all live a life and have great ways of seeing things if we all just live like Tori. We will all become great people if we just took our time out of our day for someone else to help them with their faith in God or even if it's just holding the door open for another person. You never know what just small things can do for a person because of what they're going through.

Tori had a great soul. She would always be there for me either coming to see if I was okay when I had my seizures, or if I ever needed someone to talk to. She spread the word of Jesus and she always had a smile. She's made sure all of Joe's friends were okay and made sure if we needed anything at all, she was there!

We would all be a little bit better if we just live like her. Spread the world for everyone to talk to someone about the good faith.

Live like Tori!!!

Our family would like to thank you so much for your kind words and prayers since we lost our beautiful Tori. We appreciate the many thoughtful cards, wonderful meals, and donations that made it possible for us to stay by her side at the hospital round the clock. It's a humbling thing to actually feel someone praying for you. Because of your prayers, God has allowed His comfort and peace to sweep over our family once again and help us through this time of loss. We are all so very grateful that we have God's promise that we will see Tori again. And when we do, I'm sure Jesus and Joe and many of our family will be by her side waiting to welcome us to Heaven. We pray that you will be with us there one day, as well. Please continue to pray for Waylon, Tristan, and baby Taylor in the coming days. We know Jesus and their Mama are watching over them closely.

The Sheeley Family
Eric, Belinda
Ethan, Jacob, Elly
Waylon, Tristan & Taylor

GRIEVING ALONE

I'm having a little alone time today. I don't think I've been left alone in a long time. I'm just now realizing the impact of that. I think Satan really feels like he can defeat me when I am on my own. He is probably trying to pick on me right now, while I am alone with my grief and most vulnerable.

I'm sure other people experiencing grief have felt the same. But while we may be apart from people or loved ones, we aren't really alone. We are praying, and that draws us nearer to God. We need to talk and reach out to people as much, or perhaps more than we usually do. Lean on your spouse, your church, your friends.

So, while grieving, if you feel alone, or claustrophobic, step outside and see the handiwork of Almighty God today. Give yourself this time just to take in the details of nature and what God has given us. And you will know that you're not alone.

God gave us a promise through His son Jesus...
"For I shall be with you even until the end of time."

Never alone.

— Belinda

TEARS SHOW STRENGTH

For those who think that tears are a sign of weakness, and you don't want folks to see you crying, let me set you straight on that.

Tears shed for a loved one are a sign of the greatest strength of all—love.

When we lose a loved one, all the love we still have in our heart for that person has nowhere to go when they're gone. So, every now and then, it comes out in tears. And those kinds of tears, my friend, are a badge of honor. Especially for parents who are grieving their children.

— Belinda

THEY WILL KNOW US BY OUR LOVE

When Tori's son Tristan was an infant, we had a horrifying experience with him.

Tori was such a good mother. She was so in-tune to what her children needed and while she was firm with them, she also doted on them as well. She recognized their every mood and I am so thankful to God for giving her that gift.

EVEN AS A NEWBORN, TRISTAN WAS ON A GOOD BABY SCHEDULE.

Tristan and Waylon woke around the same time and napped during the day. They both had an 8 p.m. bedtime schedule. He was sleeping well throughout the night as a newborn! But one night, when he was just six weeks old, something went wrong.

At 10 p.m. that Saturday evening, Tristan screamed out in his sleep! Not a regular baby cry, not hungry cry, not a tummy ache cry, but a tortured scream! Tori went to him immediately and when she went to pick him up, she realized he was so hot that his skin was burning her hands! She immediately undressed him, put him in the car seat and headed for their local hospital.

> At this point of the story, I always stop and thank the Lord that I wasn't in charge of this mission. I would have wasted time putting him in the tub to cool him down, done Tylenol drops and tried to soothe him. But not Tori – she knew this was major. And I still believe that God put that drive in her to take action.

The doctor on-call at the hospital in Bardstown had seen meningitis before, thankfully, and began treating the baby before he even ran the spinal test. Once confirmed though, he immediately sent them to Louisville hoping to save our boy.

Tori called me at 4 a.m. Sunday morning to let me know that Tristan was being taken by ambulance to Kosair Children's Hospital in Louisville. He was a very sick baby and my heart nearly stopped when she told me he was diagnosed with meningitis. She told me to come on to the hospital to be with them, but she prepared me that he may be gone by the time I got there. Not words a Granny wants to hear about her newest grandson!

I raced to the hospital, of course, not knowing what I would find there. I knew I had to be there for my daughter, so I steeled myself against the tears that wanted to fall. I remember praying the entire drive there. This was our surprise baby! This was the baby that we didn't count on, but we were so blessed and excited to get him! Even his brother Waylon was already enjoying taking care of him and reading and singing to him. Nothing could happen to our little guy!

When I arrived and found my way through the maze to the NICU, Tristan was still fighting for life. There were IV's and machines the likes of which I have never seen on such a little baby. Over the next twenty-four hours we found out that he had a strain of meningitis that was so rare that there were only two other cases of it in the

United States. Our baby had his own infectious disease team of eighteen doctors that patrolled him around the clock—and all eighteen of them congregated in the room each day for the next eight weeks to update us on his progress.

THE NEXT EIGHT WEEKS WERE LONG, BUT GOD BLESSED OUR BABY AND OUR FAMILY SO MUCH.

Tori never left the baby for the first several weeks, but finally we were able to make her go across the street to get something to eat for thirty minutes and take a small break while one of us sat with the Tristan.

Our grandchildren are blessed with several sets of grandparents! We all took turns coming down to sit with him so Tori and Matthew could rest and get a little break here and there. Tori didn't want the baby left alone, and we didn't want to leave Tori alone! The nurses laughed at us and said we were on the "rotating grandparent schedule." But it worked!

Tristan was getting better and stronger finally. The problem was getting meds and fluids in him because his tiny little veins kept bursting after a few days on the IV. He was running out of viable veins! We had so many folks praying for him, and God was so good. As the last of his meds went into his last IV, the vein gave way. He received all the medication. And he was finally ready and able to come home!

During our stay at the hospital, Tori and our family must have made an impact on the nurses, doctors and other families in the NICU.

Many commented on the kindness, the strength and the bond of our family. Many of them asked us to continue to pray for them. We didn't set out to be missionaries on this trip to the hospital, we were just our regular selves. But when your normal way of living glorifies God, other people can see that without you saying a word. And that is what happened there. I remember a song from my childhood, "They will know we are Christians by our love." God used us to reveal Himself to others.

I LOVE THE KIND OF MOTHER TORI WAS.

She was the loving, caring, fierce Mama Bear kind of mother we all need in our lives. She was a teacher, a leader, a protector and the love of her children's lives. Waylon, Tristan, and little Taylor were gifted with that special kind of mother. While she was taken to Heaven sooner than we would have preferred, she left some amazing memories and inspired a lot of people to be a better version of themselves. I so look forward to seeing her again one day soon when I am called home.

NEED JESUS

Nothing drives a parent to the feet of Jesus faster than their children. Whenever there is a problem, an emergency, a health crisis, or a death, the immediate normal response is "Jesus, Help Me Please!"

Unexplainable peace comes from Jesus. Sometimes healing, sometimes answers, always comfort.

Don't be afraid for your children and grandchildren to see you need Jesus. Let them see you lean hard on Him for everything—big situations, as well as the small things in life.

Teach your kids that God knows each one of us individually, personally. Because of that, we need to try each day to live our best God-approved life. Do what He would want us to do. Say the kind, good things He would have us say. Be a witness with our actions, not just words. Show people that we love them, because He loves us.

Don't just tell this stuff to your children, let them see you LIVING it!

— Belinda

THE CEMETERY

When I was a little girl, I was so afraid of going to the cemetery. I suppose I had watched a few "unauthorized" scary movies at some point and it left an uncomfortable impression in my mind.

Through the years, family members would pass away, and I came to realize that my fears were silly. The cemetery was simply a resting place until Jesus returned to gather everyone up with Him.

After my father died in 1997, my perceptions changed once again. I didn't want to visit the cemetery because it was the saddest day of my life, to date. I didn't want to think of him there. That was only his body there. My daddy was in Heaven, so I didn't want to visit him in that sad place. I chose to go to the happy places we had visited together and remember him there.

WHEN JOSEPH DIED, AN INTERESTING THING HAPPENED.

I very carefully chose his grave site in our small town where his friends could stop by easily. From his site, you could see a beautiful red barn on a hill surrounded by hay waiting to be baled. In the distance, I could see his middle school where he had attended and played baseball. It seemed perfect for Joe.

I didn't want to wait for the grass to grow up on its own over his plot after the burial. I wanted sod so it looked pretty right away. Mr. Mason was kind enough to give us the sod and told me it had to be watered *a lot*!

My sweet husband, being the innovative thinker he is, rigged up my truck with a makeshift water tank and hose and off we went to the cemetery. Morning and night I watered that sod—I was determined to keep it green! I didn't want to let down Mr. Mason or Joe.

After about six weeks of watering (I was actually relieved whenever we got a good rain), I realized that, for me, the cemetery wasn't what it used to be.

After all the time I spent watering grass, which took an hour in the morning and in the evening, I realized it was a place of comfort. Not because Joseph was there, that's just his human form. But it was the most peaceful atmosphere where I could just hang out and talk to God.

A few times, I was late for my evening watering sessions and actually had to water grass in the dark. I wasn't sure how that was going to feel. Turns out that it was amazing. I know that sounds crazy, but at this cemetery, many of the grave sites have decorated with flowers as well as these little solar lights! Up on the hill where our spot is, you can look over the whole cemetery and it's like little stars are everywhere below you in a peaceful sleeping blanket of lights.

The cemetery isn't uncomfortable anymore. It's a peaceful, sweet, meditative place where I feel close to my Jesus. And I love seeing Joe's face on his gravestone—that smile just shines out at me when I see it.

~

Fast-forward one year.

I'm watering sod at the cemetery again. This time for my sweet daughter, Tori. Her babies have colored pictures for her headstone. I had them laminated so they will last a while in the weather. How can my heart feel so shattered that she's gone one moment, and then in the next, I'm filled with joy that she's with Jesus? She's with her brother, she's with her family who has gone before her. How amazing!

As I sit here, keeping grass watered, and trying to reconcile my emotions, I can feel the Holy Spirit calming me and saying, "This has been your goal for your children and grandchildren. That you all meet in Heaven and spend eternity with Me. Make sure they all know Me. Make sure they know I did everything for them."

I'm thinking as I sit here, if someone had asked me a few years ago "How do you know you're going to Heaven?", I would have answered, because I believe in Jesus, I believe that He died for my sins, I believe that He rose again, I believe that He lives and waits to bring me home with Him. After some consideration though, I think I need to take the "I" out of the equation. Because it's not from anything I have done that I am saved. This is more accurate—I get to claim salvation and go to Heaven because He loves me, He died for my sins, He rose again, He lives, He wants to bring me home with Him. Yes I believe and accept His offer—but it is and has always been His plan for me. And He did all the work. Thank you, Lord Jesus!

— *Belinda*

THE BIBLE

Mother's Day 2018

I am still trying to function as a mother for my two remaining sons on this Mother's Day. I'm definitely counting on God's strength today, because I do NOT have any of my own left. Joe is gone, Tori is gone. Oh, I know where they are, but my Momma heart is missing them so much today.

But Eric, Ethan, Jacob and Elly are ready for church and I need to get myself together. So, off we go to church! I love my husband and kids so much for being sensitive to my feelings on this day. They are laughing and being light-hearted. I know they are still hurting too, though.

— Belinda

I had been given a beautiful Bible when Tori passed away. But on this Mother's Day, I chose to carry my old Bible that Tori and I bought together years ago. We bought a pretty tapestry cover for it, and it had handles, and I just thought it was so special. I treasured it because I had gotten it with Tori and we got her one very similar. I had carried it for ages, and then tucked it away when I got a new study Bible. For some reason that morning, I decided at the last minute to pull it out and take it instead of my new one.

I made it through the music today without too many tears. Usually, I'm a crying puddle of a mess because the music just touches my heart so deeply. During the prayer, I just kept thanking God for taking care of my babies and blessing them in Heaven into His care. Still okay on the tear-check.

Then I opened my Bible and a paper fell out in my lap. I never heard anything else during the sermon. I had my own little sermon in my head.

It went something like this: "Thank you Lord so much for the love letters from my children. You knew I would be missing them today and since they couldn't be here, you allowed me to find pieces of them that I had lovingly tucked away in Your book. I know I will always miss them, but because You let me see these signs, I will not let my grief from missing them overshadow the joy of having had such special times with them."

SEE, WHAT FELL INTO MY LAP WAS A DRAWING OF A POND WITH FISH, FROGS, TREES AND JOE AND ME SITTING ON THE BANK.

It said "I love fishing with you Momma." He had drawn it during church service when he was about seven-years-old, so it wasn't an elaborate masterpiece. But to my heart this moment, it's priceless.

I started wondering what else was hidden in the pages—nothing. But, then in the inside front cover of my pretty Bible cover, I found a card from Tori! It was a Mother's Day card from her, Matthew and Waylon. I hadn't seen it in ten years.

What were the chances of my finding these things in a Bible that I hadn't carried in years? What were the chances of it being on Mother's Day?

I have been through so much, but I have been so blessed. God knows what we need all the time. He is good all the time. And His timing is perfect. Even, maybe especially, for a grieving Momma.

HAPPY BIRTHDAY TORI

October 30, 2018

Happy Heavenly Birthday sweet Tori!

There isn't a day that goes by that I don't miss you. When the phone rings, I still, for a split second, think it might be you calling… and then I remember.

I still talk to you in my dreams. And the hole in my heart still hurts so bad it makes me double over at times. I can still hear your voice in my head.

You would have been 33 years old today. You're still my best friend and I will always love you. Celebrate with Jesus and Joe and give them hugs from me. Can't wait to see you again beautiful girl.

— Momma

THE BEDROOM

There is nothing worse, as a parent, than having someone deliver the news that your child has passed away. Because Joe was in the car accident by himself, his dad and I never got to tell him goodbye and hug him one last time, but his brother Jacob got to him quickly so that made me feel better that he wasn't by himself.

THE NEXT WORSE THING, I THINK, IS KNOWING THERE IS AN EMPTY BEDROOM IN YOUR HOME AT THE END OF THE HALL WHERE ALL HIS STUFF IS.

And part of you expects him to be there too, but you keep having to remind yourself he's not there anymore. And so, your heart takes another hit, and another, and another every time you pass by there.

You think it'll get easier, and you wonder why you can't make yourself go in. What is wrong with me? It took me about a month before I could just go stand in the room. I finally let myself sit on the bed. For a minute. Then I had to get out, the feelings were still too raw.

Three months later, I was still picking up shirts and smelling them, just to have a whiff of the precious person who would never wear these clothes again.

Six months later, his scent is fading from his clothes, and I'm almost panicking that I'm losing that too! The logical part of my brain is telling me that this room and his clothes can serve another purpose. But my Momma part of my brain is screaming... Too soon still!!! Not ready to give it up!

Eight months had gone by. My husband was strong, my God is strong. I was not. So, I asked them both to go into the room with me to choose just one T-shirt to give to each of the grandkids so they can sleep in it. Just something of Joe's to give them a hug each night. That wasn't so bad since it was for the babies.

After that, and with a lot of prayer, it just seemed to get easier to ask my daughter and my sons to go in with me to see if there was something that was dear to them that they wanted to keep as a memento of Joseph.

It took a long time to let things go. And honestly, I still have a few boxes of his things that I tucked away just for me.

When Victoria passed away unexpectedly just one year after Joseph, I was faced with more boxes of clothes, shoes, and mementos. Because she had her own home, a friend of hers and I boxed up her things, divided what we could between her children, and I just held on to the rest. And held on.

Then one day, about six months after Tori died, a very dear friend and her mother-in-law took care of the rest of Joe's and Tori's clothes in a very special way.

~

A FEW MONTHS PRIOR, I WAS TRYING DILIGENTLY TO REORGANIZE MY HOME AND CONSOLIDATE SOME THINGS.

My final task was to decide what to do with all of Joe's and Tori's clothes that I had been holding onto for dear life for the past few years.

So, I took a deep breath and started emptying out drawers and filling containers with the clothes, all the while remembering each time they would wear this pair of pajama pants or that baseball jersey, this bandana in her hair or his flannel shirt with the sleeves cut out. Every single thing I put in those boxes was a memory that I didn't want to give up. I think I wiped tears on every single item as they went into the box. It was my last physical thing to hold onto, hug, smell…

I'm sure I should have done it ages ago, but I couldn't muster the strength to endure the breakdown I knew it would cause. But I prayed, and I did it. Simple, right? No, because then I just sat and looked at the boxes and bags that held all my children's last clothing they ever wore. Thinking, "Okay, you got this far, now what do I do with all this? Where do I take it?"

And that's where I was when my sweet friend, Jessie, came in to pick up my granddaughter, Elly, to play with her little Maycee. She could see I was struggling, and I shared what was in the bags and boxes. I told her my dilemma, I cried again, and asked her opinion. Jessie is such a positive, sweet soul. She is calming and has a gift of soothing people—I wonder sometimes if she even is aware of it.

But, that particular day, she hugged me, smiled, and said words that struck terror in my heart: "Let me take all that for you. I'm gonna do something with it for you."

Not soothing at all, Jessie! Until she followed up with "My mother-in-law makes memory quilts. We'll make something for you and for Tori's kids." Whew! Okay, that was comforting after all.

～

November 4, 2019

Jessie and Linda presented me with the sweetest gifts—a quilt for each of Tori's children made from patches of her clothing and a quilt for me made of Joe's clothes (baseball dirt stains included). Then, they surprised me again by bringing me a quilt of my own made from the rest of Tori's things. I never dreamed there was enough fabric for me to have a Tori quilt too!

I adore my Tori quilt and my Joe quilt!!! And Waylon, Tristan and Taylor love theirs, as well. They were in wonderment going thru and pointing at each patch and yelling "Remember when Momma wore this?"

Remember these pajama pants? Look Taylor, Momma wore this when she was gonna have you! Look Tristan, remember Momma's fishing shirt? And look at Joe's baseball jersey with the numbers! They remembered!!! And we have pictures of Tori and Joe wearing the clothes that my grandbabies are now going to wrap around them and cuddle up. Thanks to my amazing friends, Jessie and Linda, we all get to wrap up with a warm hug and lots of memories from Tori and Joe.

It's been 6 years now. I have a few pairs of their shoes still living on my shoe rack in my closet. I have Joe's FFA jacket hanging in there where I can see it. And Tori's sun hat and flip flops she wore at the beach on her last trip with her kids. I can still see pieces of them each day.

My husband and my sons still wear Joe's dress shirts to church sometimes. There are days when I wear Joe's or Tori's big sweatshirts when I'm missing them an extra bunch and need to feel them hug me.

But the quilts are so special. They have lots of memories in one big warm hug. Best gifts EVER!!! Thank you Jessie and Linda!

— Belinda

BLESSINGS

Before Joe and Tori passed away, I loved God, I trusted God, I prayed to Him, and believed in Him with all my heart.

After we lost Joe and Tori though, I found myself leaning, clinging, relying, depending on Him completely, intentionally, more than I had before—for everything—every little thing, even my next breath.

—Belinda

I knew in my head before that God provided everything I needed, but this was a whole new level of dependance. I found I couldn't function without Him by my side at all times.

In my head, and often out loud, I talked to Him through every motion of the day. I needed His encouragement to put one foot in front of the other at times.

I REMEMBER MY FIRST TRIP TO THE GROCERY STORE AFTER JOE DIED.

Because we're in a small town, I knew the store would be a challenge and everyone would want to talk and hug. I thought it would be so difficult for me. I said "Okay God, here's another thing I need you to help me get through. Let's do this!"

It was what I had thought—people hugging me, talking to me, and literally loving me through the store. Instead of being an emotional gauntlet to travel through, it was a trip of encouragement and love. It wasn't difficult at all with God by my side—it was a blessing!

I suppose that tends to happen when you ask God for every little thing through the day.

But I think God wants that kind of relationship with each of us. He wants us to know and acknowledge that we need Him. And that we want Him there for every single thing we do—great or small!

PRAYER

I hear people all the time wishing each other good luck, good vibes, sending good wishes your way. Well, folks, I'm here to tell you that stuff isn't gonna do a bit of good.

Only thing that's gonna make an impact in this world is prayer to God through Jesus' name. Prayer will make things happen, and prayer will make Satan shake in his shoes. And prayer will get you through any situation… I am proof of that.

— Belinda

TRADITIONS

This Thanksgiving I'm so very grateful that my family's traditions have given us such wonderful memories of Tori and Joe and all our loved ones. These pics are from their last Thanksgiving with us. Makes me think of Tori successfully taking over the "Cooking of the Turkey" and Joseph helping me cook the sides and the little ones sneaking bites when they thought we weren't looking lol. What a treasure!

— *Belinda*

STICKERS

It still makes me so incredibly happy in my heart when I see a truck going down the road with a "Joe Sticker" or "Tori Sticker" in their back window.

I love that Joe's and Tori's friends still do a Truck Cruise every March (and the occasional burnout) to remind me that they're thinking of my children and our family.

It is so important to a parent that other people remember their children who have passed away. I am so thankful for all these kiddos—they have brightened our lives by keeping my children's memory alive.

— Belinda

MARY'S EXAMPLE

Mother's Day 2019

I had someone tell me the other day that they admired the way I handled the death of my children—with my head held high and trusting God. I never know what to say to people when they say things like that except thank you. But, it's strength from God, not from myself. And I've had people compare me to Job in the Bible— believe me, I've thought of a few similarities there as well.

BUT, AS BIBLE HEROES GO, I'VE ALWAYS ADMIRED MARY.

She must have been such a devout believer in God for Him to trust her with His Son. What a task to know that you're raising the perfect Savior.

And then to just absolutely fall in love with your baby and watch Him grow and live a perfect life.

And then watch as He gets abused, ridiculed and killed in the most horrific way.

And you're on the sidelines—and you can't help—and you can't stop it – and you're panicking.

And then somehow God gives you the grace to make it through.

And God has people around to escort you away from it all.

And God gives you a calm peace that no one can explain—just that you handled it with grace.

I didn't have to endure all that Mary went through, but I always loved the grace with which she carried herself. And I prayed God would let me have just a little of that to get me through my loss.

I love Jesus and I am so thankful for my salvation thru Him. But, just now, on Mother's Day, I'm also so very thankful for Mary's example of what a mother can endure and still carry on and make a difference for others.

Happy Mother's Day to all the Momma's out there—and prayers for the ones who are missing their babies today.

SECRET JESUS

You know the game, Secret Santa, that you participate in at Christmas time? How nice it feels to sneak and give someone a little something unexpected and then just sit back and enjoy the blessing they are receiving? And you also receive a blessing for giving it! But then in Secret Santa, at the end of the week, everyone finds out who their Santa was and the magic is over.

I THINK IT WOULD BE BETTER TO BE "SECRET JESUS" TO PEOPLE.

I have had my sons and my granddaughter help me with this. When COVID forced us to quarantine, there were so many elderly and needy shut-ins in my little community who couldn't get out to the grocery, or who were ill. A few young men at the Christian church near us asked for volunteer cooks to provide meals for those folks during that time.

My family discussed it, and we had plenty of food to share. I contacted the fellas and every Monday and Thursday they would stop and pick up eighteen prepped meals from our house. We had the best time cooking together for everyone! But we made the guys promise not to tell it was us doing the cooking those days. I wanted our family to be "Secret Jesus" to those families.

Well, it's a small town, and after a while we kind of got busted. Folks found out it was us cooking and sent thank you cards, one sweet couple even brought us some flowers from their garden when they felt it was safe for them to get out and about.

But it was such an amazing lesson for us that we don't need that pat on the back from people when we do good deeds. We need to be Jesus to people, just because we love Jesus.

Now every day, when my granddaughter goes to school, I know she secretly does something sweet and kind for someone. And it's just between her and Jesus.

"Help somebody without telling everybody!"

PHOTOGRAPHY

In 1998, my husband and I moved to Mt. Eden and were excited to put Tori and Ethan in a private Christian School in Shelbyville. I wasn't employed at the time, so it was a financial struggle to make the monthly payments, but we felt this was where the Lord wanted our children.

I was fortunate to get to spend time in Ethan's first grade classroom as a helper. One of the projects we planned for Christmas, was a little book of pictures of the children for them to give to their parents. I have always loved taking pictures, so this was my time to put that talent to work!

The little picture books were a hit – the parents loved them. And after Christmas, the teacher asked me an unexpected question…

WOULD YOU PLEASE TAKE MY DAUGHTER'S SENIOR PICTURES?

I didn't know what to say! I had never taken pictures like that before! But okay, let's give it a shot. She wanted to pay me, but I had no idea what to charge for such a thing. So, I just told her that would be her daughter's graduation gift from me—if they turned out good.

Well… they turned out great! We made enlargements and copies for family members. I was so happy, and relieved, that she liked what I gave her! Now, you would think that at this point, it would cross my mind to give a career in photography a thought! But no. Not yet.

After Ms. Evans showed off her pictures with the other folks at school, I began receiving several phone calls for senior picture shoots as well as family photo shoots.

I'm telling you, God opened a door for me for a career! The problem with me was, I wasn't a very good listener. So, God had to practically drop-kick me through that door.

MY PHOTOGRAPHY CAREER BEGAN BEFORE I EVEN REALIZED WHAT WAS HAPPENING!

I was frantically trying to figure out how much to charge people and what to offer. Where to print pictures, where to get a proper camera and flash and other equipment. Finally, I realized that God had provided for me what I didn't even know that I needed. A way to have a job from home that would let me spend time with my babies and pay for school and manage to have extra money.

I really didn't do much advertising; it was mostly word of mouth. Soon I was shooting sports team photos, weddings and on and on. I was having so much fun! I was meeting so many people in my community and loving what I was doing—what a blessing! God put me in situations where He could use me.

My gift also allowed me the opportunity to grow my family. After Jacob was born, we decided to try one more time to have a little girl. Joseph was born the next May (that's a whole other chapter)! Seems Tori was destined to be our only girl in a house full of boys!

God continued to bless my business. For the next twenty years the folks of Taylorsville would call me the "Picture Lady." In hindsight, I realize that the real gift was having my family close to me those twenty-plus years. When I think of the memories we made… well, it's just that very gift from God that is sustaining me through losing two of my children. I have few regrets about how our time was spent.

Looking way back, I was five years old when I took my first pictures. I thought it was just magical! I loved it from then on. I loved the artistry of it. And I loved the preservation of the special memories on paper. It wasn't until I was thirty-two years old that it turned into a career for me.

When the Bible tells parents to "train up a child in the way they should go", I know it is referring to their relationship with Jesus. But I also think God is telling us to help our children to find their talents and help nurture those talents so that they may use them as adults.

It could be photography, nursing, engineering, farming, cooking, parenting at home—the list goes on. But if you love what you do, you can be sure it is your gift from God. He means for you to use your gift to glorify Him. When you find the path that He wants you to follow, the one that makes you happy, it won't seem like work at all.

MISS YOU
MARCH 16, 2020

March 16, 2020

Oh, my sweet girl – I miss you every day! It's strange to think it's been 2 years that you've been gone. So much has happened in our family, but God gives us strength to keep going and doing what He wants us to do.

I'm so thankful that you accepted Jesus so that we can know you're in Heaven waiting for the rest of us. What a comfort for a parent! I am also thankful that God placed such loving people in our lives to help with Waylon, Tristan and Taylor. Of course, they miss their Momma – and we talk about you often to help them remember. It would make you happy how well loved they are by everyone.

And you my sweet girl are loved every single day. And while I will always miss you, I love seeing you in the eyes and smiles of your children. As long as I have them, I will have a piece of you here.

Missing you just a little extra today. I look forward to being able to hug you again one day soon.

Love,
Momma

PSALM 23

This is a text I sent to Pastor Chad on January 3, 2021.

Just thought I'd share –

Last night I had the most overwhelming feeling come over me. I'd been thinking so much about Tori and Joe, and it popped in my head that I had literally walked through the valley of the shadow of death. Which then led me to recite Psalm 23 in my head.

I had memorized it in the 6th grade for Bible Drill. I still haven't forgotten it 44 years. It still holds up and I love it! And then while I was lying in bed thumbing through Facebook, I found the church page and found out what your sermon was covering this morning – Psalm 23. Wow! I just thought that was cool!

— Belinda

THREE YEARS

March 16, 2021

Tori has been in Heaven for 3 years today.

Just missing you a little extra today, my sweet girl! Your babies are growing up beautifully, and I know God lets you look down and see them. I know they bring joy to you in Heaven just as they bless everyone here. Miss Taylor is still your little mini-me, and Waylon and Tristan have turned into handsome, wonderful young men. I still catch myself picking up my phone to call and tell you something – isn't that silly? But I still feel you with me, so I guess that's why. Three years without you – hard to believe. I live for the day we're all together in Heaven. In the meantime, watch over us all. We're always thinking of you and Joe! Love you Sissy!

— Momma

NICOLE'S DREAM

May 27, 2022

Eric and I were standing outside our house this afternoon, weeding the landscape, I heard a truck coming up our road. And it honked at us! Not unusual at our house—we get that a few times a day out where we live. But I didn't recognize the truck until it stopped in front of the house. Stan and Nicole had stopped to show off their new little grandbaby! We hadn't seen them for almost three years, so it was super nice to get to visit with them. Their son, Dalton, was Joseph's first best friend in kindergarten and they remained best friends until we lost Joe in 2017.

We talked about babies, and Joe, and goats, and trucks. And then Nicole got serious and said she needed to tell me something that happened to her.

— Belinda

NICOLE TOLD ME SHE HAD A DREAM ABOUT TORI AND JOE AWHILE BACK, BUT SHE DIDN'T KNOW WHAT IT MEANT.

She was so happy to have seen them both! She dreamt that she was sitting at her desk doing paperwork at the lake resort where she worked a few minutes from our house. She heard the door open, and when she looked up, there stood Joe and Tori smiling at her! Her heart was so happy to see them both!

Nicole asked, "I'm so happy to see you, but what are you doing here?" She noticed they were each carrying a box. Tori smiled and said "We are getting ready for a party! We have party stuff in these boxes."

Nicole wanted to ask about the party, but instead said, "Tori, Joe, I have to tell your Momma that I saw you! She's going to be so happy!!!" Tori said, "Will you please tell her I love her and I can't wait for her to come with us?"

Then, Tori, being Tori, used her elbow to punch Joe in the arm and said, "Joe, don't you want Nicole to tell Momma something from you?" Nicole said she just had to laugh at them, still acting like brothers and sisters do. Joe just smiled his usual big old smile and said, "Sure! Tell her I love her and Daddy a bunch! And I miss 'em."

Nicole got up from her desk and went and hugged both of them around the neck. She said that was all, no more words were spoken, just smiles. And then, it was gone.

It was a beautiful experience she wanted to share with me. But to her it seemed very real, like they had truly spoken with her. And the dream didn't fade away as some dreams do. She had waited days, maybe weeks to share it with me. And it was as vivid in her mind as she told it as when it happened.

God's messages to us can get a little confusing sometimes. You see, a few weeks prior to Stan and Nicole's visit, I had been looking at those very resort cabins to possibly have a birthday party there for Tori's little girl, Taylor. At first, I thought, maybe Tori was trying to tell me—"Sure Mom, have Taylor's party there!" I was just happy that Nicole had such a cool dream experience and shared it with me!

But then, one day later…

~

May 28, 2022

I got a phone call this afternoon from Matthew and Erin. My grandson, Tori's oldest boy, Waylon, was going to be Baptized on May 29, tomorrow! They wanted to be sure we could all be there. I got goosebumps then, and I have chills again as I write this. It dawned on me that Heaven may not celebrate parties for little girls' birthdays… but they must surely party and celebrate when someone accepts Jesus and is born into the Kingdom of Heaven! That's the party they were preparing for! That WAS the reason for the celebration! That realization was awesome! I called Nicole and told her what I finally figured out! It was kind of a head-slap moment for me – I knew then I was not a good interpreter of dreams lol.

— Belinda

I believe as sure I'm sitting here, that God used my children to speak to Nicole. Just another of His awesome, precious ways of letting me know that my babies are His. They are with Him, but they can also see us when wonderful things happen in our lives. Even though I miss them both so much, I allow God to fill me with happiness and find the joy only He can offer.

I pray that other parents who have lost children let God reveal Himself in similar ways. What a blessing to be on the receiving end of a message from above.

Nicole messaged me this after our phone conversation.

Belinda, I am so incredibly blessed and honored that I was able to share! So glad they came to visit me, it was truly special to me. I will always have a special place in my heart for those kiddos. I think between God, Tori and Joseph, it was His plan that we went down y'alls road at the perfect time. God's timing!

~

May 29, 2022

I didn't get to speak to Waylon until right before his Baptism today. We got to the church a little early so I could pull him aside and tell him my story. As I was telling him about Nicole's dream, I could see his eyes welling up with tears. He and I hadn't had a real heart-wrenching cry together since his Momma's death. But he and I both had one outside the church that day – when I got to the part that Waylon's decision to follow Jesus was the reason for the celebration. They were happy tears, though, as I told him that I knew his Momma and Joe would be with us today in that church watching him come up out of that water! When he stood up out of that water and looked out at me, it was the happiest and most peaceful I had seen him in ages. And it was the best message delivered, in a most unusual way!

— Belinda

A CONNECTION

May 1, 2023

I am gearing myself up to go to the funeral visitation in a few days for a young man from our community. I had not met him before. He was a senior this year —2 weeks shy of graduating with his class. Nathan died in a one vehicle accident, just like my Joseph. He was ejected from his car and thrown to the ground, just like my Joseph. How could I not go to the funeral? How could I NOT be there for that poor family?! Part of me wanted to hide at home, but the stronger part of me said—you're going!

— Belinda

So, I reached out blindly on Messenger to Nathan's mother. We weren't Facebook friends, but I took a chance that she may see my message. I could at least let her know who I was, and that I had been in her place exactly six years and one month previously. I pressed send at 3:47 p.m. and prayed she'd see it eventually.

Dear Kathryn: My heart is breaking for you right now. And though you probably don't know me, I have been in the place that you are at this moment. We lost our 16-year-old son, Joseph in 2017 in a single car crash. Then exactly one year later, in 2018, we lost our 32 year-old daughter to an unexplained heart attack/infection.

After Joseph died, I remember trying, needing to sleep, but not wanting to… because I knew I would have to wake up and realize all this wasn't a nightmare. I remember seeing faces of loved ones, dear friends around us, and thinking, I pray they never have to know this feeling. So many emotions, so many tears, so many ups and downs, so many prayers.

God is the only way I was able to cope. Talking to Him and accepting His comfort gave me strength. And knowing that my son was with Jesus was the greatest comfort of all. You may never see this message. But I will still be praying for your heart to be able to find the peace you need to be able to function day to day. And you, your husband, and daughter will remain on our prayer list. If ever you need to talk, please reach out to me.

Sending hugs. Belinda

I couldn't sleep well that night—you tend to re-live events in times like these. And then, late in the night, my phone dinged.

And it was her!

She let me know real quick that she *did* know who I was and she wanted to meet me soon!

Belinda, thank you so much for reaching out. I know exactly who you are, and what you've been through with working in the cafeteria at TES for the past 7 years. We know some of the same people. In the next few weeks, I would really like to meet you. Get some guidance and pray together. Nathan's grave is in the same row as your beloved children. The only thing getting me through this is my faith.

Oh Kathryn! Hold on to that precious faith! When Joe and Tori died, I was determined to use our tragedy to show people how strong our Lord can be and how they could be saved and know Jesus. And how He blessed us so much. But when you make that commitment, Satan will pick at you and test you. That's when you sic God on him!

I remember feeling so low one day at the hospital when we decided to take Tori off of life support. I just yelled "Why does God keep taking my babies from me?!" And He answered me! And it took my breath away! And His answer was – they weren't really ever mine. They were His – I just got to borrow them for a sweet, special time.

So, I know where they are now. I know I will see them again. And you'll see your baby again too. I believe God was ready for Joe and Tori to come home because they had finished their work here on earth. And I believe that about Nathan.

His passing, though it's an excruciatingly, painful loss, is about to get used by God to win a lot of high schoolers to Jesus. I really believe that! There is joy in that! And that's what gets me through every day for the past 6 years. I try to look for the joy in everything – even in my loss. And God makes it possible.

Let your heart listen. Satan will try to use your sadness and grief against you. But so many people are praying for Jesus to comfort you… you have to allow Him to do just that. You will feel the peace from Him – I did. And it was strange but amazing knowing that God was working in me.

I've had people tell me they admired my strength with all we went through. But you've already found out, it wasn't my strength, but the Lord's. I don't even try to take credit for that strength, because on my own I'm not sure I would have survived. I am so thankful you have Jesus in your heart to guide you through this pain.

I will see you soon – when you feel like visiting. Know that I will help any way I can. Even if it's just sitting at the cemetery or in your living room. I'll be praying for you all! Sending love. Belinda

Belinda!!! God led you to type out exactly what I needed to hear! I might have to quote you at the funeral. My husband is writing his eulogy. Not speaking it. I have been on Facebook reading all the comments and getting caught up on texts for the past few hours and I haven't cried a bit. It's so comforting knowing what the community and his fellow students thought of him. And I found myself wondering why I can read all these comments and messages and I'm calm and feel comforted. You're exactly right! I'm letting the Lord comfort my heart and it's the most amazing feeling in the world. Your son, Jacob, approached Chad at church on Sunday to give us a message that he is willing and able to talk to us when we are ready. I would love for him to talk to Natalie about how to cope as a sibling. I hope to meet you at the service. I could really use a hug from you.

I will surely be there for you sweet lady! Tell
your husband and daughter I send my love
and prayers for them as well. See you soon!
And try to sleep if you can!!!

PASTOR CHAD

I sent this text to Pastor Chad at 3:33 a.m. on May 2, 2023.

> Just wanted to let you know I'm praying for you. Once again, you'll be preaching a funeral for what sounds like a very well-loved young man. I know you will do an amazing job and God will give you the words to reach out and touch so many lives. Sounds like Nathan laid the ground work being such a good friend to so many. Perhaps it'll be like when Joe passed, and some will make a decision to accept Jesus. That's my prayer.
>
> I have been in touch with Nathan's mom, Kathryn. We messaged back and forth somewhere in the night around 3 a.m. I had reached out to her yesterday. I've never met her so I felt a little awkward. But in the night, she messaged back – and I think she's in about the same frame of mind that I was. A little numb and leaning hard on Jesus. It works. I'm anxious to meet her – she said she can't wait to hug me. I have a feeling we will become friends.

> All this just made me re-live our experience and reminded me how much you helped guide us through. And I wanted to let you know that we love you and are so thankful for you and your family! You're all very dear to us!

Did you notice the time I sent this? I surely didn't mean to send my pastor a text and wake him at 3:33 a.m.! I thought—I'll just type what I want to say to him and send it later this morning. But my fingers had a mind of their own and my thumb hit send! Yikes!!! I felt so bad thinking I would be waking him. But he texted back right away.

Later that afternoon, he asked me, "How did you know I was up this morning?" I just looked at him kind of confused. He said, "When you sent the text early this morning, how did you know I was up? And you knew exactly what I needed to hear? I was at the church in my office praying for the words to come to me to help this family."

I guess God meant for me to hit send.

NEW FRIENDS

Wednesday, May 3, 2023

I'm going to meet Kathryn today. This is not the way I want to meet a new friend. Her teenage son was killed in a one vehicle accident on a back country road late Saturday night. Sounding familiar? Yeah, she is living my nightmare. And my heart is totally devastated for her. I don't even know her yet, and my mind is crying out for her comfort and peace to deal with this horrific dream that we can't wake up from.

But God is way ahead of me. And He's telling me He's going to need to use me. I've been there for other grieving Mommas. But this one is different for some reason that I don't know yet. I feel a connection to her, yet we've never met.

— Belinda

I stood in a 2-hour line at the funeral visitation with my husband, son, and granddaughter. We were all wondering what to say, how to act, what to do. And then my pastor walked by and stopped to talk to us. He asked if we're okay—but honestly, we were really not sure.

He asked, "How can you be here? After what you've been through, what made you want to be here? Isn't this painful for you?" Eric and I just looked at each other. "God wanted us here. We're supposed to be here to serve this family tonight. They just need to see us. See for themselves that we made it through this, not once, but twice! And God was still holding us together! To see that they can get through this awful time."

We waited… and we waited. Finally, we were next to visit the family. Even though we hadn't met before, Kathryn knew who I was and she knew our story of losing both Joseph and Tori only one year apart. She had been waiting for us. And when we locked eyes, all the tears we had both been holding back for days rushed out. We leaned into each other and I have no idea how long we stood there. Folks were probably thinking we were losing it, but quite the contrary. We found solace in one another. I needed her and she needed me in that moment.

They had tons of people there to love them, pray for them, encourage them, hug them. But no one can imagine, or even come close, to the feeling of losing a child in that way unless they've been through it themselves.

We are both in the club now. The worst-best club there is for a mom. Our children aren't with us anymore (the worst), but we know our children are in Heaven with Jesus (the absolute best).

We are going to be good friends, I believe.

ANOTHER FUNERAL

Thursday, May 4, 2023

Today is Nathan's funeral. I've been to way too many funerals for young people these past several years. My heart hurts for their family, each and every one of them. But, especially the Mom. She is shattered in so many pieces, that she doesn't even want to be put back together... I know.

But God will guide her along the way, and she will be strong again. Because she knows Jesus. And she will want her son to see her doing good things to help other people through their hurtful times like this.

It's hard not to re-live my own hurt that I felt at Joseph and Tori's funerals. But today is about Nathan. I honestly didn't know any of them until this tragedy. But God led Nathan's father in writing a beautiful eulogy, and between the meaningful words, and beautiful photos, I feel like I got to know Nathan. Wow! I just kept thinking that he and Joe would have been great friends, and that Tori would have had another honorary brother.

Then it dawned on me. Joe and Nathan are now friends, and Tori is likely chasing them around, enjoying taking care of both of them.

Nathan's Mother asked if it was alright that they chose a grave site just a few spots over from Joe and Tori. I said absolutely it's okay! I couldn't think of a better place, it's so beautiful there. So, our kids are neighbors, here and in Heaven.

— Belinda

THE IRISES

This text began just after Joe passed away between myself and my friend, Nancy.

MAY 2017

> Belinda, I truly believe Joe changed those flowers so that I would take notice of them. I only knew him for a moment, but he impacted my life forever.

> That's beautiful, Nancy! I love thinking they changed color for Joe!

A few days ago, I received this text and picture from my friends Nancy and Paul. They live in the home next to where Joe had his accident. Nancy and Paul were there for Joe and Jake – they ran out of their home and sat with my boys until help arrived. Nancy tells me she planted these flowers years ago. These Irises have come up and bloomed a deep purple every year – until this year. The month after Joseph's accident. And now they're white. I don't believe that's a coincidence. Thank you for sharing this with us, Nancy. Very sweet to think they may have changed for Joe this year.

— Belinda

(Just for the record, they bloomed purple again for the next 5 years!)

Until...

MAY 12, 2023

Nancy just sent me a photo of her purple iris patch. It bloomed white this year. Now I really don't think it's a coincidence at all. Here's an updated photo.

— Belinda

Here is the text conversation with Nancy and myself.

> Haven't seen a white one in this spot since the year Joe passed. Always thinking of you, Belinda, and sending love.

> You're so sweet! I was just thinking about you and your flowers – actually every day this week! I just love that we had such a clear message from above. What a gift! I'll be forever grateful for you sharing that with me.

> I love, love, love messages! I can't see a red headed woodpecker without saying hello to Joe! When I saw these, I just knew I had to share with you. I knew Joe for the briefest of moments, but he will forever live in my heart. I will forever be connected to you and your family in a way that is unexplainable. Sending love to you all as his birthday approaches.

In March of 2019, I received a message from Nancy that gave me goosebumps. She has mentioned to me before about seeing a red-headed woodpecker and calling it Joe, and she talks to it like it is Joe. She finally shared why she associates that little bird with my son…

> Here's a Joe story for you… I sense Joe around our home a lot! I talk to Joe randomly and I've come to associate a red-headed woodpecker as a sign from Joe. In the fall of 2018, my daughter and son-in-law were in a really bad car accident. Well, it could have been bad, but they walked away with minor scrapes and bumps. I drove by the accident scene awhile afterwards and was praising God for keeping them safe.

Not 10 seconds after I said this, I saw a red-headed woodpecker on the edge of the road just sitting there looking at me. Not in a tree, but on the road where I would obviously see it. The bird sat there and looked at me as I drove past it. I got a complete sense of acknowledgement that this was Joe letting me know he was there and protected Abbey and Luke that day. His way of telling me "Thank You" for me being there with him right after his accident.

I'm so thankful for Nancy and Paul for being there for both my boys that awful night. How amazing to think that God placed Godly people right where they needed to be in that moment. What a blessing! What a comfort that my boys were surrounded by loving people taking care of them.

FINAL THOUGHTS FROM BELINDA

How do you know you have God in your heart?

I felt He was there with me when I got baptized at nine-years-old.

I felt He was with me when I went to a Christian school for seven years.

I felt He was with me as I went to church each Sunday for most of my childhood and through my teen years.

I felt He was with me when I prayed.

But in my teen years and early twenties, I decided to let the world tempt me, and I did things that normal, rebellious young people do. I got away from church because I didn't want someone reminding me that I was doing things God would not approve of. I didn't "not believe in God," I just pretty much ignored Him. The prodigal child perhaps.

But then I had children. I knew how I wanted them raised. I knew how I wanted them to act. And I knew what I had to do.

We got back to church—my husband and I surrounded ourselves with Godly people that would teach my kids *and* us about the Bible, about Jesus! The Bible tells us to "Train up a child in the way they should go, and when they are old, they will not depart from it." That was so true for me, and I appreciate my parents being firm in their guidance. It has served me well.

When my kids were little, I knew I had to give my whole self to God for Him to give Himself to me. I didn't know that someday soon, I would have to give the children back to Him. He's been preparing me for serving Him. He's been preparing me for sacrificing back to Him.

When I finally gave everything back to Him and said "It's all yours, Lord—all I have is Yours to use," *that* is when I felt the Holy Spirit moving in me. *That* is when I felt I could understand His answers to my prayers. And *that* is when, at my lowest, darkest times in my life, God gave me His strength and made me a witness for Him and not a victim of my sorrow.

I find more every day that the things of this world make me shy away from them—I don't *want* to do things that would disappoint Jesus.

When the Holy Spirit is in you, He makes you want *more* of His joy and *more* of His goodness. He makes you want it for others as well. Helping and serving others now is a goal for me each day. Even if it is just a little something to help a neighbor. I love doing things for other people—not for their appreciation, but to glorify Jesus. To make folks happy and to spread His joy and love. God blesses my heart so much whenever I cook for someone and send them a meal. And I especially love serving people from behind the scenes. I am not serving them for my glory, but for His.

I don't mean to make myself sound so holy—I am so far from perfect that it often astounds me. But I ask Jesus to forgive me, and He does. And I try again to do better tomorrow.

I know that everyone deals with their grief in many different ways. But when I serve Jesus, it fills my heart with a feeling that is so much stronger than my sorrow for my children. It makes me remember that my ultimate goal is to see Jesus in Heaven and hug His neck and thank Him for His amazing love for me. And then I'm going to go find my babies and hug them so tight!!! It's going to be incredible to be in Heaven with so many loved ones.

I pray that any person who reads this gives their heart to living for Jesus. And for those who don't know Him yet, that you will consider a relationship with Him. I pray that everyone who has lost someone close to them can see forward past this life to Heaven and look forward to being face to face with Jesus and then being reunited with their loved ones. The time is drawing closer when we will all be together again. Parents, grandparents, brothers and sisters, friends, it's our job to make sure everyone we know, knows Jesus. I can't think of a better way to spend eternity than with Him and those we love.

— Belinda

FRIENDS FOR LIFE

After Joe passed away, our family decided to offer a memorial scholarship for his school. We would choose a student who was not necessarily going to college, but perhaps entering a trade or straight into the work force. The main idea of the scholarship is that you are a loving, caring friend to those in your school and community.

The Joseph Lee Taylor Sheeley
"Friends for Life" Scholarship

The Joseph Lee Taylor Sheeley "Friends for Life" Scholarship has been established by the family of Joseph to acknowledge that student who is outgoing and friendly, has a strong work ethic, loves the outdoors, and is a friend of the community.

Joe's absence still affects so many in our community, and the family would like to offer the scholarship to that individual who demonstrates characteristics that Joseph valued.

Be kind to everyone in all walks of life, be honorable, be

respectful, and love our community and everyone in it and, every day, make someone laugh. Most of all, let God's love shine through your smile.

Joseph loved Spencer County and, it seems, Spencer County loved Joe, as well. Joe considered everyone he met a "friend for life." Because of Joseph's faith in the Lord, we are blessed that we can still be his friend beyond this life. What a wonderful promise God has given us that we will be reunited once again.

Support the Joseph Lee Taylor Sheeley Scholarship Fund with a donation. Contributions can be sent by mail to:

Belinda Sheeley
PO Box 335
Taylorsville, KY 40071

ACKNOWLEDGMENTS

My mother, Sandy Mayer, who encouraged me to even begin writing my story. She and my father taught me to rely on the Lord for all things. She taught me the stories from the Bible, sang me the songs, and took me to church. She built the foundation on which I live.

My sister, Heather Heller, who is such a prayer warrior. I'm sure she prayed me through my grief as well as through writing this book.

My grandmother, Norma Webb, who was with me in the darkest times of my life and kept me focused on the Lord.

My pastor, Chad Goodlett, who stood by my family and encouraged us all. Each time I shared an experience with him, he believed in me. He told me so many times, "You should write a book about what you've been through." Finally, I did it, friend!

Our crew of dear friends, Pam and Mike, Betsy and Bill, Leslie and Daniel, Lori and Nick, Ashley and Matt—they constantly supported us, kept us busy, kept us doing things, kept us going places. God surely placed them in our lives!

My dear friend Erin, who is now the step-mother to two of my grandchildren. I love that you are in our family now. And that you and Matthew have given us sweet baby Jasper to add to our family. Thank you for reading this book with my grandson. The book review from you and Waylon was the one that made me believe I should keep moving forward. Thank you!

My Bible study gals, Starr and Vonda. The constant prayers you send up on my behalf, the sensitivity you show when you know a song or a sermon may make my tears fall, are so appreciated. You ladies make me a better person.

Our Spencer County Community—I don't know how to ever thank every person in an entire county! But, here goes... literally thousands of people showed up for us to support us in some way or other over the past several years. Whether it was at the funeral home, a meal, a prayer, a hug at the grocery store, or spinout marks on the road in front of our house to remind us they were thinking of Joseph and Victoria. I don't know anywhere else where people would have loved on us the way this community has. I'm so thankful God put us right where we are. You all have blessed us so much!

And Stephanie, I love that we became friends through this project. You made me believe in myself when I thought I hit a huge road block. Without a doubt, God led me to you. You've been amazing!

ABOUT THE AUTHOR

 Belinda Sheeley is a mother of four, grandmother of four, retired photographer, caretender of way too many goats to keep up with, animal lover, new author and longtime believer in Jesus.

Belinda has maintained focus in her life with the help of her husband of 33 years, Eric, and their four children, Victoria, Ethan, Jacob, and Joseph. Together, they chose for her to operate her photography business from their home so that they could have more family time. She believes this opportunity was a blessing from God and was vital to instilling Christian values and having precious years raising her children.

After the loss of her youngest son Joseph, and then one year later, her daughter, Victoria, Belinda began journaling and keeping her most private, treasured thoughts and entries on paper. However, after seeing others attempting to navigate grief, she felt she may be able to help if only she shared her story with them. Her message in this book is about people finding Joy, the fruit of the Spirit, as they navigate through loss and grief. She wants others to be able to take their own situation and use it to glorify God's holy name. No matter how tragic the loss or how deep the pain, God can work through you. That has been the foundation for her message, her mission, and her ministry.

www.ingramcontent.com/pod-product-compliance
Lightning Source LLC
Chambersburg PA
CBHW070657130626
46553CB00005B/1736